B3032

THEATRE IN A TENT

FRONTISPIECE. Large dramatic tent used by the Federal Theatre Project in Springfield, Illinois, in the 1930's.

THEATRE IN A TENT

THE DEVELOPMENT OF A PROVINCIAL ENTERTAINMENT

William Lawrence Slout

Bowling Green University Popular Press
Bowling Green, Ohio 43403

Library of Congress Catalogue Card Number: 72-186635
ISBN: 0-87972-028-X   Clothbound
        0-87972-029-8   Paperback

Printed in the United States of America.

This study is dedicated to my father, L. Verne Slout, who in life personified the spirit of the tent show: stake driver, manager, press agent, and Toby comedian; who faced the vicissitudes of trouping with the philosophy, "when they sit in the blues, I play to 'em."

TABLE OF CONTENTS

PREFACE

REPERTOIRE TENT SHOWS, WHICH BEGAN TRAVELING AMERICA IN
the last half of the 19th century and continued well into the 20th,
brought summer entertainment to thousands of small towns in all
parts of the country. From 1900 to 1920 tent shows increased in
number to form a rather sizeable industry. Development was inter-
woven with many of the popular amusements of the early century
until, carrying the traits and the scars of such diversions as the circus,
moving pictures, vaudeville, Chautauqua, and touring opera house
companies, the repertoire tent show emerged as a distinct form of
rural theatrics.

Tent show troupes traveled with canvas theatres in which they
performed a repertoire of plays and vaudeville. For the most part a
summer activity, hundreds of companies operated in their own
limited territories, returning to many of the same towns year after
year, and usually staying a week in every locale, offering a different
program each night which consisted of three and four act melodramas (or comedy-dramas) with vaudeville sandwiched between
acts.

The word "repertoire" is used throughout this book instead of
the more familiar "repertory." I am adhering to the preferred spel-

ling by repertoire performers. "Tent shows," when not otherwise qualified, signifies dramatic companies performing a repertoire of plays under canvas. Tents were utilized for a variety of amusements including medicine shows (which were sometimes repertoire companies), moving picture shows, vaudeville shows, circuses, musicals, concert companies, and any number of one-night stand dramatic troupes (*Uncle Tom's Cabin, Ten Nights in a Bar Room, Jesse James*, etc.); but when these are referred to in the text, the distinction is made clear. Although repertoire tent shows were commonly called "rep shows," "tent rep," or simply "rep," I have remained with "repertoire" for consistency.

My purpose is to show the development of the typical tent show. The tent show grew from the opera house repertoire companies of the late 19th century as they adopted the tent used by the circus and adapted it to resemble a portable theatre. The first two chapters establish the nature of both the small town opera house and the repertoire troupes that performed there. Eventually repertoire managers were faced with financial and operational pressures stemming from the use of these indoor facilities; Chapter III defines some of the conditions responsible for an increase in outdoor activity. Chapter IV shows the development of the canvas theatre from its use by early circus troupes to its ultimate design for dramatic productions, as the simple round top tent grew into a simulated opera house. The progressive growth of repertoire under canvas, from early stirrings to the prosperous era of World War I, is outlined in Chapters V and VI. With the emergence of hundreds of shows throughout this period, a rural audience, formerly remote from staged dramas, was created. Plays were written to satisfy this new body of theatre-goers; and special emphasis was placed on certain popular themes relating to the small town and the farm. The dramatic literature of tent repertoire is explained in Chapter VII. Out of this literature grew a lovable stock character, Toby—the traditional rustic of low comedy. Toby's historical lineage and a conjectural reenactment of his 20th century birth are described in Chapter VIII. The final chapter deals with business practices peculiar to outdoor operations, many of which were borrowed from the circus. The use of the canvas portable theatre by repertoire troupes that had customarily performed indoors created a distinct type of show business which by 1920 had become well established in physical shape and in practice; and for the remaining years, tent shows held closely to this mold.

CHAPTER I. THE SMALL TOWN OPERA HOUSE

THE LAST THIRTY YEARS OF THE 19TH CENTURY HAVE BEEN CALLED
the golden age of the Opera House. Rapid expansion of railroad
mileage following the Civil War furnished the means for touring
companies organized in New York and other large cities to add heretofore inaccessible towns to their itineraries, breaking up long jumps,
and thus making the touring more profitable. Increased theatrical
activity spurred small town businessmen into building more adequate
structures to house the performances of these troupes. Methods of
operation developed by these touring companies were carried over
and used by repertoire troupes when they began performing in portable canvas theatres.

Theatre construction throughout the United States from the
Civil War until around 1910 increased proportionately to the addi-
tions in railroad mileage. Nine thousand miles of railroad tracks in
1850 had in ten years grown into a national railway system of around
30,000 miles. Railroads assumed a new importance through the transportation necessities of the Civil War. During the war years, for example, freight tonnage on the Erie and New York Central railroads
combined to exceed for the first time that of the Erie Canal. Westward expansion following the hostilities fostered the increase in

track mileage to a total of 93,000 by 1880. Concurrently, opera house construction occurred in nearly every village and hamlet and continued at a rapid pace (with the 1890's showing the greatest activity) into the first decade of the 20th century, creating the vast theatrical network that was known as "the road."

Nearly every town on a major rail line found a need for an opera house. By 1896 the number of theatres in cities large enough to profitably accommodate national touring companies had increased to an estimated 1,300. Many were in communities of from two to five thousand population. Smaller places had some manner of theatre, but seating was limited and audience potential insufficient to lure first-rate touring companies performing for high admission prices. Local managers of small town theatres had to be satisfied with booking an occasional repertoire company or a third-rate one-night stand amusement.[1]

The use of the names Opera House and Academy of Music gave the structures an image of respectability—theatre being in ill repute. The practice was by no means new. When in 1787 a Philadelphia law prohibited theatrical performances, the Southwark Theatre was advertised as the Opera House Southwark. The subterfuge was compounded by calling plays performed there "Spectaculum Vitae" and by presenting musical comedies under the guise of opera—there being no restrictions on opera. *Hamlet* was represented as "a Moral and Instructive Tale as exemplified in the History of the Prince of Denmark"; *The School for Scandal* as a "Comic Lecture in five parts on the Pernicious Vice of Scandal."[2]

Further public disdain for the theatre occurred in Brooklyn in 1856 when that city was being considered for the site of a playhouse. Opposition by the townspeople forced the new structure to be called the Academy of Music. There was, as well, public resentment from the use of a front curtain because a curtain "is intended to conceal something and concealment suggests impropriety."[3] So the desire not to offend members of the community persisted in the small towns as new buildings were erected and dignified with formal block letters placed on the cornices that read: Opera House.

Opera houses were sometimes municipally owned. Orleans, Nebraska, although "small and remote," maintained a theatre "that reflected the public spirit and modernity" of the community. Located in the center of a village square and surrounded by tree-planted grounds, the building, by ordinance managed by the town marshall, "paid a handsome percentage on the investment."[4] Such places were symbols of local pride, an indication that the town had passed its stage of early development and had settled down to being a solid, forward-looking community. A local opera house was often a thing of beauty, designed to outdo the theatres in close-lying towns. The building was used for such functions as lectures, political rallies, home talent shows, dances, and high school graduation exercises. Frequently, it was constructed to house civic facilities as well. For example, the opera house in Vermontville, Michigan, erected in the late 1890's, was placed over a firehouse and council chamber. The Laurium Opera House in northern Michigan's copper country, a three story structure featuring a clock and bell tower, housed the fire department, while the second and third floors were arranged into theatre, ticket office, and dressing rooms. Most opera houses that doubled as community centers were built with flat auditorium floors and movable seating that could be pushed aside or stored, leaving space for dances, basketball games, and other such functions.

Eventually, leading businessmen came to realize that the operation of what was sometimes the town's only place of amusement could be profitable.[5] Privately financed theatres, managed by local merchants or professional men, were usually designed to accommodate commercial stores on the ground floor; the second story theatre was entered by a wide wooden stairway, distinguished by the innumerable initials carved in the wainscoting, or scratched on the plaster. Local management was occasionally a part-time effort, for the businessman-owner neglected the theatre in favor of his main source of income; and although the manager was interested in turning a profit on his investment, he was too often ignorant in the ways of theatre operation. For these and other reasons, opera house management could be a short-lived occupation.

To create a typical small town opera house, one would begin with a facade facing onto the main street, grandiose compared to the buildings on either side, and distinctive by the name of the theatre appearing at the cornice—City Opera House or Academy of Music. Often the edifice was ennobled with the addition of the word *Grand* to the title, such as Bonner City *Grand* Opera House. At the street level a double-doored entrance would be flanked on either side by a store or office to allow for a constant source of income from a building that might receive only an occasional rent for its theatre. The entrance would open into a wide stairway leading to a second floor lobby or hallway where there was a box office, and perhaps other rooms facing onto the street that might be rented out. Inside the theatre, chairs would be arranged in customary blocks. The type of seats could vary from plain kitchen chairs to elaborate, overstuffed opera chairs. If there were a balcony, it would be relatively small, with benches for seating. The stage would be raised to a higher level than in modern theatres to insure better audience vision, since there was no tiering of the main seating area. The stage floor, adhering to tradition, would be placed at a slight incline toward the rear. There would be little wing space and stage depth. Dressing rooms (probably two) would be small, dimly lit, dirty, and cold. The theatre would be stocked with drop curtains and wings depicting a street, a prison, a parlor, a kitchen, and a woods, as well as a few smaller set pieces such as rocks, a stump, and a set house, all serviceable for the conventional locales called for by the popular dramas of the day. A few pieces of plain, rickety furniture would be all in the way of properties. The front roll curtain would be painted to represent a foreign landscape or a scene taken from mythology. On either side of the proscenium opening, panels of local advertisers would be exhibited. An out-of-tune piano would be pushed to the side in front of the stage; and at one or more points around the auditorium would be the familiar pot-bellied stove—in winter, stoked to a red heat. If the theatre were built after 1895, chances are it would be lighted electrically; otherwise, gaslight or kerosene lamps would supply the illumination.

Audiences and performers around the opera house circuits found few comforts. The seats were hard, the theatre was too hot in the summer and too cold or drafty in the winter, acoustics were generally bad, and stage quarters were cramped and dirty. Actor Will H. Locke recalled that many of these upper-story theatres had no rear exits to be used in case of fire or for occasions when there was necessity for "strategic retreat." The practice of the Josh Henderson Stock Company, with which Locke was an actor, was to place a ladder against the wall under a back window to service the various emergencies that came not infrequently to touring companies.

Stock scenery of wings and drops became an all too familiar sight to the townspeople. The editor of the *Berrien County Record* of Buchanan, Michigan, suggested in an 1889 article that the Rough

Opera House management "shoot the woodpecker on the stump in the rural scene, or make him catch the bug he has been chasing for the last ten years. . . . The citizens of Buchanan have seen the actors walk over the tops of the houses in Charlie Collins' street scenes until Baron Munchausen's yarns have no charm to them. If there be anything the American people enjoy it is an occasional change."[6]

One way of improving sight lines was to place the rear seating on platforms rising tier by tier toward the back of the house. Bent's Opera House in Medina, New York, used this method. The last five rows were elevated eight inches each. Also, five rows of tiered seating were arranged along either side of the theatre, requiring the auditors to look sideways to the stage. These raised sections represented the most expensive seats—seventy-five cents for the rear sections, fifty cents for the sides, and thirty-five cents for the level portion of the auditorium.

As a rule, the small town theatres were poorly managed by local citizens who knew little about the ways of theatrical production. Theatre attendance in many communities was insufficient to warrant full-time attention. Bookings were occasional and the theatre was dark throughout the summer months. Too often theatres were left to "run themselves." Will Locke related an experience on the Josh Henderson show that illustrates this point. Henderson, who had booked a town on short notice, arrived to find no advertising posted. So Locke and Henderson looked up the theatre manager who was the local banker. When asked about the lack of show paper anywhere in town, the banker replied that he had been too busy to bother about it. Disgusted, the men took their advertising, still in the bundle in which it had been shipped, and left for the opera house, a barn-like building situated on a side street. When they arrived they found the seating area almost completely filled with baled hay. Plows and other farm implements were stored on the stage. There was no piano in the place, only an old organ. So, as was frequently the case, the actors improvised.

We were unable to find a musician who would play the thing. Our little ingenue could play "Over the Waves" and I could peck out with one finger "I Owe $10 to O'Grady." So we set the groanbox on the stage and the first entrance and for overtures all that week Maude played "Over the Waves," and for cue music

I pecked out "I Owe $10 to O'Grady." We changed plays every night, but there was no change in the musical offerings.[7]

Dressing rooms were usually dirty, poorly ventilated, and badly furnished. "The actor who secures a looking glass that is not cracked or a wash stand that is not in eminent danger of toppling over," wrote one trouper to the *Dramatic Mirror*, "is indeed considered fortunate, and as for a carpet on the floor, that is a luxury seldom found."[8]

This is not to say that all small town managers were haphazard in the operation of their theatres. The astute businessman, interested in providing the community with good amusement, could turn a respectable profit. Some managers devoted fulltime to their theatres and acquired the management of other theatres in the area, forming circuits that provided them with greater bargaining power in booking decent attractions.

Opera house proprietors offered a wide assortment of entertainments: musical extravaganzas and comic operas, such pieces as *The Black Crook, Humpty Dumpty, The Grand Duchess, The Bohemian Girl, The Daughter of the Regiment,* and *Fortunio* performed by the Worrell Sisters Burlesque and Opera Bouffee Company, Lisa Weber's Celebrated English Blondes, Mlle. Ninon Duclo's Sensational Blondes Revue, Oate's Comic Opera Company, Holman Opera Troupe, Ford's Juvenile Opera Company, Liliputian Opera Company and other like groups. Minstrel shows were perennial attractions. Tambo and Bones cavorted for West's, Dockstader's, Culhane's, Chase and Weston's, Hi Henry's and numerous lesser known organizations. Although minstrelsy was in decline by the 1880's, there were still well over thirty recognized companies touring the country. Concerts were popular, featuring the United States Marine Band, Ellery Royal Italian Band, Sousa's, and Gilmore's. There were solo musicians of every variety including Blind Tom, the talented negro pianist; Ole Bull, the Norwegian violinist; pianist Herr L. von Myerhoff; and Irish prima donna Rosa D'Erina.

One-night stand dramatic companies, including the never ending flood of *Uncle Tom's Cabin* and *Ten Nights in a Bar Room* troupes, were the meat and potatoes of every theatrical season. The Broadway hit play, which after a New York run was organized for provincial touring, was especially appealing. The "name play" could usually do well without the services of a high-priced actor. With a successful New York show, bookings were easy to acquire; local managers competed for dates. On the other hand, there were promoters who, with a few dollars, organized road companies of unknown plays. With no title to sell, these producers had to accept bookings rejected by the first-rate attractions. Frequently, this meant long jumps of continuous one-night stands. Many of these companies were formed in the Middle West, designed to appeal to a rural audience; one such was *Si Plunkard*, with which actor-manager John C. Lewis toured for some twenty years in the title role.[9]

The successful shows out of New York were dependent on the shrewdness and theatrical awareness of the traveling manager who represented the metropolitan promoter. The managers had to guide the company through the varied obstacles encountered once the company began the tour. A good traveling manager possessed an extensive knowledge of the profession, a familiarity with the types of audiences encountered in the numerous areas, experience in working with railroad rates and time-tables, and an acquaintance with the host of local managers.

The company functioned on a strict time schedule. Trains had to be boarded at precise minutes; baggage had to be readied for pickup and carted to the station and loaded onto baggage cars. William H. Crane observed that train conductors would not "cause a 'lightning express' to tarry even to suit the tardy convenience of a Booth or a Bernhardt."[10] Frequently, companies travelled by "milk and vegetable" trains, making poor connections, many stops, and taking round-about routes. Such service often kept the members of the company in travel from early morning until arrival at their destination, just in time to walk onto the stage for the performance.

By today's standards the actor's life on the opera house circuit was not easy. For some forty weeks a year he lived out of a trunk, a favorite being the Taylor Theatrical Trunk—guaranteed for seventeen years. If he were in one of the principal roles, he was allowed one trunk for the theatre and one to use at his lodgings; if he were one of the lesser performers, he might have to make do with merely hand luggage. Sometimes the actor was allowed to have his "hotel trunk" unloaded only two or three times a week.

There was always the real danger of financial failure that could leave a company stranded in some out-of-the-way place with no funds. Crane estimated in 1892 that approximately half of the productions sent on the road by experienced promoters never finished the season.[11]

In a letter to the *Dramatic Mirror* the same year, Henry DeLussan complained that it was not uncommon for a troupe to be abandoned without notice in some strange town "without means of support for a single day." He told of such an incident occurring in Reading, Pennsylvania, which resulted in the actors' trunks being seized and the actors being sent to jail:

Such an abandonment, too, sometimes influences to crime. People made desperate by want are disposed to steal rather than starve, and many a woman who otherwise would have been blameless has been lost because of being absolutely destitute with no hope of aid.[12]

He went on to state that during the past year he had seen six companies stranded in this manner. Wildcat managers, boasting of an "angel" but operating on a "shoestring," found no difficulty in hiring actors for provincial touring. Actors were said to be "the most gullible, near-sighted and unbusinesslike set of mortals under the sun." They signed with an unscrupulous manager, were abandoned, and "cheerfully signed again with the very same manager, only to have their experiences repeated."[13]

Throughout a large part of the golden age of opera houses there were no central agencies to systematically route the innumerable traveling shows in their annual treks across the country; consequently, bookings were conducted in an amazingly informal and frequently haphazard manner. Local managers secured their attractions by corresponding directly with producers or by going to New York City in the summer lay-off period to negotiate with them personally. But mail was slow; with a show remaining only one night in a place, a letter of inquiry was often weeks in catching up with the itinerant manager. Frequently, traveling companies ignored such correspondence. A complaint to the *Dramatic Mirror* by Thomas M. Thatcher, manager of the Gem Opera House, Somerset, Kentucky, illustrates this point:

Inquiries for open time, written on striking stationery blazing with brilliant colors, and setting forth with circus extravagance the alleged merits of some new aggregation in the dramatic field, are received by the poor house manager, who at once replies giving all necessary information sought, and rushes his letter off by first possible mail. He then patiently waits weeks for a booking that he never secures. He does not, in most cases, even receive a reply to his letter. . . . The managers of traveling companies too often regard the man at the other end of the wire as of no consequence whatsoever. He is generally classed as a butcher, a livery man, an insurance agent, a pawn broker, a real estate dealer, a "hoss" doctor, or as one in some other line of business, that has the management of the Town Hall on the outside, in order, chiefly, that he and his family may attend the "show" free.[14]

One-night stand organizations arranged their dates well in advance of their tour. Consequently, it was more satisfactory for the local manager to go to New York during the summer period, when seasonal heat forced the closing of his theatre, where he could personally conduct his booking arrangements. If the trip were successful the manager left New York with the better part of his winter season arranged for. Some of the companies that he had booked would never hit the road, for various production reasons; other companies would most probably fold before the winter was well along. Such disappointments were part of the business, expected, and later remedied through correspondence.

The negotiations were conducted in and around the theatrical center of the time, Union Square. Since very few producers worked out of permanent offices in those years, discussions took place almost anywhere, on park benches, in barrooms, hotel lobbies, or just on the street. Managers milled about seeking out the preferred productions, evading the less desirable promoters until all else failed, listening to rumors, boasting of the drawing power of their theatres, bargaining, renewing friendships, and generally putting their winter seasons together piece by piece, much as one would put together a jigsaw puzzle. Alfred Bernheim described the general hubbub as "a sort of hybrid between a county fair and the New York Curb market in the days when it still operated in the open air on Broad Street."[15]

Rarely was there a contract used to bind booking agreements; but most agreements were lived up to. After all, each party needed the other to continue in business. It was in the best interests of the one-night stand producers to keep their companies on the road as long as a profit could be realized. To do this the producers required the good will of the theatre managers, not only the ones that provided the most lucrative dates but also those who operated theatres needed to break long jumps between profitable engagements. On the other hand, the local manager had an obligation to his patrons to furnish them with the best possible season. A breach of contract on either side amounted to an inconvenience and sometimes a financial sacrifice. Word of bad faith spread rapidly, a fact of life that served to keep both parties in line.

Nevertheless, there are many recorded instances of ill booking practices. Road companies sought the theatres that were located in what was called "good show towns." If an opening occurred in one of these better houses after the season was under way, the traveling manager sometimes cancelled a poorer date for the more promising one, occasionally without informing the losing house manager of this intention. To insure against open dates, the house manager sometimes booked more than one attraction for the same night, figuring that at least one would make an appearance. Surprisingly, for a booking system as slipshod as the one just described, undesirable situations occurred less frequently than one might expect.

It seems obvious that from every aspect of the theatre the opera house circuit was a rough avenue of operation. The theatres were uncomfortable—small, dirty, either too cold or too hot—ill-run, and often unprofitable. Seating was inadequate to support first-rate companies in many of the small town houses; consequently, patrons had to settle for inferior entertainment or stay home. Because of difficulties in filling out a complete season, local managers frequently turned to the small repertoire troupes which were barnstorming the hinterlands. These companies could perform for one or two weeks in one place without repeating a play; and if the ten-twenty-thirty cent admission brought in meager box office returns, it at least helped pay theatre maintenance.

CHAPTER II. OPERA HOUSE REPERTOIRE COMPANIES

THE PROLIFERATION OF NEW THEATRES, WHICH ALLOWED COMBINATION companies to tour in great numbers and to fill nightly engagements through relatively short jumps from one place to the next, encouraged an increase in repertoire companies between the 1860's and 1910. Early barnstorming troupes that operated on the policy of presenting plays wherever there was an audience and staying as long as this traffic would bear them— sometimes playing through the winter season in one theatre in much the manner of a stock company, and then striking out with the coming of warmer weather for short engagements in the small communities of the region—found it plausible to function in a fashion similar to the one-night stand companies. With enough plays for a week's engagement, a company could encounter a new audience weekly without changing any of the pieces in its repertoire. Engagements could be booked into opera houses on dark weeks, between major one-night stand shows, allowing many local managers to have almost continuous occupancy of their facilities. The increasingly popular appeal of melodrama, coupled with a switch to lower admission prices, spurred a boom in the repertoire field that reached its peak in the 1890's and continued into the early years of the 20th century.

There is no necessity at this time to record the history of the

stroller; it has been set down by many writers of theatre. It is sufficient to note that the opera house repertoire companies, and the
tent repertoire companies that followed, are descendants from the
colorful and hardy strolling bands that date back to the time of
Shakespeare, when the "most conservative of all players," as Alwin
Thaler called them, carried the Elizabethan touring traditions from
one generation to the next and, eventually, into the 18th century.
The life style of these ancient barnstormers differed little from our
turn-of-the-century American troupes.

They left long trails of debt behind them, and played more than one rather
scurvy trick upon their hosts, but they brought the old plays and the new away
from the cramped quarters of London's theatrical monopoly into the furthest
corner of the provinces. They kept England merry England still, besides crossing
the ocean and establishing the theatre in the colonies including America.[1]

The strolling tradition was brought to America under the auspices
of bankrupt London manager, William Hallam, and under the direction
of his brother, Lewis. The small band of English actors encountered
inadequate theatre facilities; with only three or four structures designed
expressly for dramatic presentations, the troupe was forced to perform
in empty stores, upper rooms, or courthouses. Sometimes there was no
way to utilize the meager scenery they had so painstakingly carted across
the Atlantic. And, performed by a small troupe, the large cast shows of
the period seemed ridiculous; Mrs. Hallam, for example, played Juliet
to her son's Romeo.

As the frontier moved westward, barnstormers followed close
behind. There can be only admiration for such strollers as Ludlow
and Smith, the Jefferson and Chapman families, and all of the obscure
companies that braved the dangers and discomforts of the wilderness
to bring a crude bit of amusement to the western settlements. After
1850, when mining fever had populated the far country, the lure of
the silver dollar brought more and more troupes into the newly developed regions. John S. Potter trudged his dramatic company cross-
country in a wagon to become one of the theatrical pioneers of the
West. His advance agent preceded the show on horseback, and hung
one-sheet advertising on trees and rocks, guiding the troupe to its
destinations. They performed in mills, attics, hotel dining rooms,
and town halls. In Sebastopol, California, a town containing little
more than a store, a blacksmith shop, eight saloons, and a hotel,
the company improvised a theatre in the hotel garret. The stage

of rough planks, enclosed with horse blankets, had a large American flag as a front curtain. Footlights were devised by placing candles in beer bottles; and beer kegs supporting boards supplied the seating. Potter's experiences are typical of the barnstorming tradition carried forward by the opera house repertoire troupes. From the days of the Hallam family until the establishment of "the road," actors experienced makeshift facilities and a makeshift existence, but the strollers' instincts kept theatrical touring alive and supplied a heritage for the acting generations to follow.

In this chapter we are talking about dramatic troupes with a repertoire of plays extensive enough to accommodate a nightly change of bills for a period no shorter than a week at prices of ten, twenty, and thirty cents. This does not include musical comedy companies that functioned in a similar manner, but usually demanded admissions of at least twenty-five, thirty-five, and fifty cents; nor does it include companies that toured with a repertoire of Shakespearean or operatic pieces. We are concerned with popular priced melodramas presented in repertoire, appealing to small town audiences who wanted nothing but entertainment. Clayton Hamilton described those who attended cheap melodramas as "workaday people to whom . . . nothing noteworthy ever happens," demanding elements in the plays "in which surprising and startling adventures will happen not only to the people on the stage but to themselves."[2]

Dramatic repertoire, as we have just defined it, came into popularity sometime in the 1880's. Assessing the changes in theatre in Lancaster, Pa., for the year 1886, Felix Reichmann made the following comment:

Two observations strike us immediately: the prices were lowered, the average is now thirty cents, and the language of advertisements is more aggressive: "A dynamite cartridge of fun," "a laughing cyclone," "a dollar performance at thirty cents," etc.[3]

Popular prices and sensational advertising were the earmarks of a melodramatic repertoire. It is quite probable that price reduction to ten-twenty-thirty was in part responsible for the surge in repertoire interest that continued for the next twenty odd years.

Although it is agreed that the popular price policy was inaugurated in the 1880's, people cannot agree on who was responsible for the change. In a letter to *Billboard* W. L. Richmond credited A. R. Wilbur with bringing ten-twenty-thirty to the Middle West: "The old managers were dumb-founded and predicted a speedy downfall for him."[4] On the other hand, Will S. Beecher voted for Geroge A. Hill, manager of People's Theatre Company; and Walter Nealand claimed Isaac Payton. Once prices were reduced, the ten-twenty-thirty fare became totally identified with dramatic repertoire

By and large, dramatic repertoire was a week-stand operation. Except for Sunday, when most theatres were dark, the companies performed a different play each night; however, many of the troupes went out with literally dozens of pieces prepared, which allowed them to vary their offerings according to the tastes of the various communities.

Selection of plays was limited by the number of characters, scenic demands, and royalty considerations. As we shall see later, royalties were of minor importance, since most companies never bothered to pay them. If dramas required more characters than there were actors in the troupe, actors simply doubled and tripled parts. Such doubling was commonplace with small companies. Marian Spitzer has indicated the extremes to which this sort of thing was carried in reporting that in one troupe the spectacle *Quo Vadis* was performed with a cast of seven. It is quite possible that the use of the cross-over beard—which actors slipped on to cross to the opposite side of the stage when theatres had no provisions for crossing out of audience view—was originally inspired by the doubling necessities of these small organizations. As for scenery, the large companies carried complete changes of sets and featured this fact in their advertising. The small companies made do with a minimum of shifting, carried little or no scenery, and used the house sets of the various theatres in which they performed.[5]

The plays were much the same from one company to the next. Popular pieces throughout the hey-day of repertoire included *Fanchon the Cricket, Camille, The Hidden Hand, The Two Orphans, The Octoroon, The Silver King, Kathleen Mavourneen, Hazel Kirke, The Celebrated Case, East Lynne, The Lady of Lyons,* and *The Sea of Ice.*

To attract the unsuspecting public to plays they had obviously seen all too often (and to avoid royalty payments) managers habitually changed titles. Repertoire actor Charles R. Phipps recalled that *The Phoenix* was performed under the various titles of *Risen from the Ashes, In Old New Orleans,* and *Back from the Grave. A Noble*

Outcast was called *Jerry the Tramp, The Convict's Daughter, The Vagabond, The Wanderer,* and *Master and Man.* One time when Phipps was passing out handbills in a store, a lady said to him, "Young man, I'm going to the show tonight; but if this play is about a tramp and his daughter, I'm going to demand my money back."[6]

Nearly all companies offered vaudeville between the acts of the plays. For the smaller companies it was a matter of hiring actors who could double parts and specialties. The larger companies, operating in cities where entertainment competition was a factor, carried from four to six feature acts. The use of vaudeville served to "fill the time" while the stage was being set. To offer a complete change each night and matinee the specialty performer needed at least eight separate routines. One season Waite's Comedy Company featured the Williams' Musical and Specialty Company, a group of seven people performing on mandolins and guitars. Charles K. Champlin toured in 1907 with as many as eight special acts. And George M. Fenberg is said to have used such high-class head-liners as Henri French, the Colby Family, and the Keatons, with each act getting $250 or more a week. In explaining the popularity of repertoire, E. E. Meredith stated that many 10-20-30 companies gave a better show than the seventy-five cent one-night attractions "and threw in a vaudeville bill that would do credit to any of the smaller circuits."[7] The specialties were an important feature of tent repertoires from the outset; which, similar to the Italian interludes of the Renaissance, became every bit as attractive to the rural audiences as the plays themselves.

Still another entertainment feature was the band carried by many of the shows. Following the tradition of circuses and Uncle Tom's Cabin troupes, costumed and uniformed bands were utilized to publicize the dramatic company. The band concert, held in a prominent public place, was a device for attracting crowds in an era when almost every community had its own band that performed weekly at the village bandstand. One manager, whose company doubled in band, always arranged to be met at the railway station by a colorfully decorated hack; whereupon the entire troupe, with music blaring, would parade to the local hotel.

Although theatres were rapidly being constructed, accommodations were still primitive in the '60's and '70's. Joseph W. Grindley, a juvenile man with the Rex Hallman company in the '60's, recalled the troupe's playing in the Junction Theatre, (Pittsfield, Massachusetts), a banquet hall just off the hotel's main dining room. In Holly, New York, the lighting in Frisby and Sawyer's Opera House consisted of tallow candles placed in tin cans that had been nailed to the floor; and the theatre's dressing rooms were improvised by curtains. When W. J. Gross was an actor for John S. Langrishe in 1869, the theatrical accommodation for the company in Cedar Creek was a cellar. Later, when roads were still difficult to travel, Langrishe and his actors left the show wagon at the mouth of a gulch, packed the equipment on horses, and walked the six miles to Bear Gulch where they performed in a butcher shop for two weeks.

John McFarland, a touring manager before there were many railroads in the Middle West, hauled his show about in a red wagon, playing everything from *Hamlet* to *Jack Sheppard*. "Opera Houses!" he remarked, "We never heard the words spoken in those days, never met with it unless we were reading some foreign papers. If we did arrive at some place that boasted of having a hall, we would have to look all over the town to find some person who had the key to unlock it, then had to sweep it out ourselves and find some way to light it up at night." Members of the company took handbills and canvassed the town, knocking on doors and lecturing to the occupants on the merits of the troupe.[8]

With the improvement in theatre facilities, as towns became larger and more able to support touring attractions, repertoire activity became more varied. The Emilie Melville Company appeared at the Pence Opera House in Minneapolis in 1867 with a group that performed *The Hidden Hand, Our American Cousin, Fanchon the Cricket, Somnambulist, The Comical Countess,* and *Camilla's Husband.* The same year the Rachael Johnston and J. R. Healy Company performed *The Hunchback, East Lynne, Lady Audley's Secret, Leah the Forsaken,* and *Ingomar* on the Pence stage. In Louisiana, the James S. Charles Company was presenting "elegant little comedies" and "well gotten up and exquisitely performed dramatic entertainments" such as *His Last Leg, The Married Rake, A Loan of a Lover,* and *The Lady of Lyons.* The pieces were followed with musical interludes of singing and dancing by various members of the company.[9] In the late 1860's and early 1870's, the James A. Lord Dramatic Company was touring in Kansas and adjoining states. Composed of some twelve to fifteen performers, the troupe presented a repertoire of *Uncle Tom's Cabin, Rip Van Winkle, The Hidden Hand, She Stoops to Conquer, The*

– 16 –

Ticket-of-Leave Man, The Sea of Ice, and *Under the Gaslight.*

There was a marked increase in repertoire organizations on the road by 1870. The Old Reliable Company, carrying twenty-five people, featured Helen d'Este and J. G. Stuttz in such plays as *East Lynne, Leah the Forsaken, Ten Nights in a Bar Room, Fanchon the Cricket, Camille, Cynthia, Ingomar, The Lady of Lyons, Fazio, The Hidden Hand.* The Wilmington *Post* judged Miss d'Este as "a careful student of human emotions, and a fine portrayer of them." She was said to have received strong support from a "mammoth company" that were " 'dead letter perfect' in their parts and correct in their costumes and stage business."[10] The W. H. Crisp Dramatic Troupe was a popular southern organization. Captain Crisp's wife and three daughters were part of the company that equalled "any usually to be seen in the large cities."[11] The first company to play in the new Grand Opera House of Wilmington, Delaware, was the Caroline Richings Bernard players, featuring Mrs. Bernard and a leading man by the name of J. W. Wallack, Jr. Their 1871 repertoire included *Daisy Farm, Rob Roy, As You Like It, Cuckoo Song, The Man in the Iron Mask, Bonnie Fish Wife, Don Caesar de Bazan, Hamlet,* and *Oliver Twist.* The Thorne Comedy Company toured in North Carolina with a repertoire of *Kathleen Mavourneen, Rip Van Winkle, Ten Nights in a Bar Room,* and *Fanchon the Cricket.* The scenery, painted by the company, was described by the *North Carolina Citizen* as "decidedly handsome." About this time, the Langrishe Troupe was a leading company in the West. Leadville's *Daily Democrat* labeled manager Jack Langrishe, "Colorado's favorite comedian," and called him an actor who gave "a chaste and superior class of amusement." Langrishe was working the mining camps of Colorado as early as 1869, in places such as Georgia Flats, Montgomery, and Buckskin Joe. Along with his leading lady, Miss Phosa McAllister, he performed *Streets of New York, London Assurance, The Octoroon, Othello,* and *Serious Family.* Langrishe had moved on to Deadwood by 1876, "with a wagon load of accessories and an extensive repertory," where he became a great favorite.[12]

One of the most successful companies of the '70's and '80's was the Martin Golden troupe, with twenty people and "a fine band and orchestra." As was often the case, the company did not bill a town ahead of its arrival. It was customary in those days for the "orchestra boys" to "program the town." The residential areas were divided into sections; and every morning at 9:30 each orchestra member was assigned two billboys with instructions to continue billing until the 11:30 parade. Former band leader, Clarence Fry, remembers the company playing over a store building owned by a man named Dunn in Denison, Texas, since no opera house had been erected at that time. "Dunn's Dungeon," as the place was labeled, had no chairs, stage, or scenery. Golden rented one hundred chairs for reserved seats and placed planks over beer kegs for the general admission section. Candles furnished the illumination; and for a special blackout effect, they were blown out by members of the orchestra.

Repertoire leading ladies increased in popularity during the 1880's. For example, Ida Van Courtland, Cora Van Tassell, Edna Paige, Lillian Lyons, Jesse Mae Hall, Madge Tucker, Lillian Sackett, Marie Kinzie, Eunice Goodrich, Clara Mathes, Maud Henderson, Evelyn Gordon, and Flora DeVoss all toured with troupes bearing their names. Katie Putnam was one of repertoire's most popular stars. During a visit to Wilmington, North Carolina, the *Daily Journal* printed a letter signed by forty-two citizens requesting Miss Putnam to take a benefit that evening in *Fanchon*. And when the actress played a return engagement the following year, she received six curtain calls, more flowers than the stage could accommodate, and the title "Wilmington's little favorite."

Repertoire was not confined to the small town opera house circuits; by the 1890's some ten-twenty-thirty managers were playing large city theatres and finding receptive audiences for their stock of melodrama. Companies which originally toured the small towns west of the Ohio River found it highly profitable to step up to the bigger theatres. The change necessitated enlarging the troupe to eliminate objectionable doubling of parts, the use of better plays requiring higher royalty payments, more elaborate scenic equipment, and the addition of feature vaudeville acts. Corse Payton and James R. Waite are typical of the repertoire managers who built their small organizations into successful, money-making ventures.

Corse Payton was one of repertoire's most colorful figures, often referred to as "King of the Ten-Twenty-Thirty." He grew up on a farm near Centerville, Iowa, the half-brother of another successful manager, Mrs. B. S. Spooner. Payton's theatre career began with minstrel shows and circuses, for which he ran away from home to sell peanuts and pink lemonade. Somewhere along the line he became a professional roller skating champion, winning many medals and making a respectable amount of money. Crediting his versatility as an actor to his experiences with an Uncle Tom's Cabin company where he played nearly every part "not excluding Little Eva," Payton boasted his range included "leading parts or genteel heavies, character old men, dialect parts, old women and, on occasion, soubrettes and leading women"; but he was most at ease in light comedy roles. His acting was a frequent target for drama critics; but, undaunted, Payton turned their scorn to his advantage by billing himself as "America's Best Bad Actor." In spite of his critics, he attracted an impressive following.

No Drew or Barrymore was ever so personally worshipped as he was. . . . His every appearance on stage was the signal for rapturous cheers and storms of applause, and when he walked on the streets he was followed by idolatrous crowds of small boys, giggling matinee girls and moonstruck matrons. He was the recipient of hundreds of gifts and countless letters, and he accepted them all with the matchless grace of an emperor secure in the adoration of his subjects.[13]

James R. Waite, known as "The Barnum of Repertoire," professed to follow the motto of "honesty, energy, and ten, twenty, and thirty cents." Waite, who first organized a company in Streator, Illinois, in the early 1880's, was one of the pioneers of the ten-twenty-thirty price policy. He describes his adoption of popular prices in the following manner:

The presidential election of 1884 had precipitated bad business, and, determining to inaugurate popular prices, I jumped from Lincoln, Neb. to Michigan and opened at ten, twenty, and thirty cents. The immediate prospect was not pleasing, but the new schedule was continued, as it has been ever since. Confining the attraction for a few years to the smaller towns, I then began to improve the company and play better places.[14]

By 1894 Waite was operating two companies; the Western unit toured in Ohio, Pennsylvania, New Jersey, and New York; the original company remained in the New England states. A year later he added Waite's Comic Opera Company and Grand Orchestra. In 1897 Waite took a company into New York City to perform at the Murray Hill Theatre under ten-twenty-thirty prices. "Although it was suggested that I should strengthen the Eastern Company for this occasion," Waite explained, "I concluded to let it remain as it was, being confident that as it had pleased over 800,000 people since September last, it would find recognition in New York. The experiment has proved successful beyond expectations, and, as far as I might judge, the people have been among the best pleased played to this season."15 The following year he advertised Waite's New Stock Company, featuring Annie Louise Ames, "The handsomest woman on the American stage," and a company "selected from the Best Stock Talent in the country." Concurrently, Waite's Comedy Company was touring the New England states with "two stirring military plays dealing with the present war, as well as two strong scenic productions."

The majority of repertoire companies performed for small communities on or off the railroad lines, toured with fewer acting personnel and less spectacular scenic equipment, experienced more difficult conditions, and were looked on with greater disfavor than the big city companies. Although the basic format of operation was the same among all repertoire groups, the small outfits are more representative of what the tent shows were to become; and, as such, are of greater interest to us here. Many of these companies toured in the middle-western states from Ohio to Kansas, which is why the performers were called "prairie actors." For the most part, the prairie actor was content to remain in small-time repertoire and put up with the uncertain employment, small salaries, and discomforts of travel. He came into the profession from a western heritage with little or no stage experience. He was introduced to theatrical life by joining a company as it passed through his home town, filling a vacancy that required him to perform with little preparation. He was often asked to learn a role per day until he was familiar with the entire repertoire. Such challenges to novice Thespians made seasoned performers of them in short order.

Frank Ketchum's introduction to professional repertoire is a common example of how prairie actors were made. As a boy, he had participated in amateur productions in his home town of Fremont, Michigan, at a time when professional actors frequently augmented their "off season" income by directing amateur plays. When Ketchum was eighteen he answered an advertisement in the Detroit *News* for a young actor—"a talented amateur would do"—and was hired by manager Frank J. Dean for his small repertoire company in Michigan. Ketchum joined the company one day just before show time. Dean, who was tending the front door, selling tickets for *Kathleen Mavourneen* soon to begin, turned over his job to the new arrival. Dean also gave Ketchum sides for the part of Father O'Cassidy in the evening's bill and suggested that Ketchum learn the role and report backstage after the first act. Ketchum followed instructions. When he arrived backstage he was rehearsed and sent on in the second act. "I can remember I spoke about half the first speech and then dried up," he wrote in his memoirs. "The curtain came down and 11:00 o'clock finally came."[16]

Luke Cosgrave joined the Grace George Dramatic Company for his first professional job under similar circumstances. Engaged at a salary of $15 a week and a promise of good roles, he embarked on a rough and tumble tour of western towns in 1886 that was a test for any "first of May." He was rewarded with such parts as Simon Slade in *Ten Nights in a Bar Room* and Francis Levison in *East Lynne*. In recalling preparation for the latter, he said, "I got a silk hat, patent leather shoes, learned to wear a monocle, and studied for the graceful charm of this polished devil—of course, letting Miss George dominate her scenes."[17]

The acting company of these small outfits was a strange assortment. The manager's wife "insisted on being the leading lady"; the character woman usually had a little girl that was billed as the "Child Wonder," and as such was featured in all children's roles throughout the week, did specialties, and continually looked like Little Eva.

The leading man often wore a blond wig in some parts, and his entrance through the center door was a studied art, surpassed only by his three-sheeting ability in front of the post office at mail time. The juvenile sometimes doubled on props. The character man had been with Booth, and expected the young upstarts to respect him. The comedian was always on the make, and kept his bald, red shellwig in a cigar box, tied with a shoestring. The general business man made his own stickum and kept it in an olive bottle he obtained from a boarding house, he owned all shades of crepe hair, and possessed seven wigs and a pair of whiskers on wire.

The heavy woman would own a black spangled dress which she wore as Kate Burke in *The Man of Mystery* and *The Woman in Black*. The general business woman aspired to be a leading lady. She was versatile, changed specialties for a week, and always made it her business to see who had the best dressing room. The heavy man could make a realistic mustache, paint scenery and banners, and do specialties. He was often wedded to an outsider, who married him so she could see the country, and to kill time she would visit from one dressing room to another, and often stirred up a little hell.[18]

It was common for leading ladies to play roles for which they were too old. Cora Warner successfully accomplished the illusion of the ingenue roles she enacted with a "birdlike voice that carried to the far corners of the hall" and a curly blonde wig that concealed a more mature set of locks. Flora DeVoss, who headed her own company for many years, eventually felt the need to issue the following slogan in her advertising: "Perhaps you knew Miss DeVoss, perhaps you knew her mother, perhaps you knew her grandmother."

Some companies were composed of an entire family. As each child grew older he was advanced from one line of parts to another, beginning with walk-on children, and going on to juveniles or ingenues, general business, and finally leads. Before Mrs. Mary Gibbs Spooner took her company into the Park Theatre, Brooklyn, for a stock engagement that lasted several years, the entire family toured in repertoire. There were two daughters and a son. Edna May played leading roles, and Cecil the soubrettes—"They were favorites in every town they visited and drew heavy box-office returns."[19] When Mrs. Spooner' son was about eighteen he wore "a handsome gold laced uniform and between acts sold photos of the family in the lobby of the theatre." He performed small roles as well; but no matter what characters he portrayed, he always wore the same "star-spangled" uniform.

Repertoire people encountered the same living discomforts that one identifies with the traditional stroller. Small town hotels and boarding houses left much to be desired. Many places would not accept actors at all. Bert Arnold, recalling his days as an actor, revealed that in some hotel dining rooms the actors were partitioned off from the other guests by drapes strung on wire. And hotel managers were always afraid—often justifiably—that the company would leave town without paying the bill. It was not surprising then when, toward the latter part of the week, a town constable appeared with a warrant to force the company manager to pay in advance. Despite such vicissitudes, the number of small repertoire outfits increased (beginning in the 1890's), performing in every small town with a hall to accommodate dramatic presentations. Places that could profitably support only a few troupes a year were visited by several, with an occasional repeat booking during the same season. Eventually, rural show business suffered from too much ten-twenty-thirty.

CHAPTER III. FROM OPERA HOUSE TO TENT

THE ROAD WAS IN DECLINE AS THE 20TH CENTURY BEGAN. THERE
were approximately 340 theatrical companies touring during the
season of 1900; by 1920 the number had dwindled to less than fifty.
E. E. Meredith wrote in 1907 that it was getting difficult to make
money with a small show. Salaries and production costs were increasing.
Theatre managers were demanding larger house percentages. Transfer
lines were raising rates for hauling baggage. Railroads were tightening
their restrictions.[1] Yet, as the century began, there was a developing
trend toward outdoor entertainment of which the tent shows were
very much a part. In June of 1897 the *Dramatic Mirror* described the
growth of summer enterprises as "remarkable."

A few years ago no venture of note in theatricals was made for the period between
regular seasons. Summer amusement schemes have been profitable, as is shown by
their multiplication in recent years; and there is every reason to believe that the
inter-season system will continue to develop until it becomes a notable factor in
theatrical calculations.[2]

Suburban and beach resorts and out-lying amusement parks, the
Dramatic Mirror noted four years later, "have multiplied . . . and

the continuously working millions that formerly had no opportunity for relaxation or amusement during the heated season, now throng the suburbs . . . where stage entertainments compete with other devices of pleasure . . ."[3]

A public interested in musical concerts and vaudeville frequented the unique outdoor roof garden theatres which were said in 1890 to be "an innovation of recent years." Modeled on the German beer garden, these places of amusement were located atop tall buildings in metropolitan centers. One such, constructed on the roof of the Guaranty Loan Building in downtown Minneapolis, gave nightly concerts two hundred feet above street level. Garden settings, colorfully lit, furnished an atmosphere for drinkers and diners to relax and enjoy the enchantment of music and fresh night air, where gravelled walks wound their "sinuous ways among the brilliant foliage and plants of the garden proper, and rustic tables and seats were strewn about for the accommodation of guests."[4]

Casino theatres in summer resorts were another popular attraction. Although resorts were being established as early as mid-century, by 1890 resort development had increased to where in May the New York *Tribune* was running eight columns of summer hotel advertising. No longer the exclusive playgrounds of the rich, resorts were now appealing to the middle class. Large resort populations fostered theatre activity and the erection of open-air facilities.

One of the most notable examples of the surging outdoor entertainment industry was the amusement park. The rapid growth of parks at the turn of the century was enhanced by the entrance into the entertainment field of the electric transit companies. Originally, these companies were formed for the purpose of getting working people to their jobs and home again. They functioned both in the city proper and between the city and out-lying communities. In about 1900, however, trolley riding for pleasure became a fad, and people of all classes availed themselves of the opportunity to get a breath of fresh air. The pleasure of riding trolleys to the end of the line and back was enhanced by the addition of a grove of trees under which was arranged a few benches, furnishing the passengers a place to alight before returning. From this simple diversion grew the idea of the trolley park. *Billboard* in 1901 reported: "Probably no amusement line has developed so rapidly the last three years as the street railway parks, or has any more profitable proposition been adopted."[5]

A typical park was located at Lake Whalom, Massachusetts, situated between Fitchburg and Worcester. The park featured a band pavilion, restaurant, swimming and boating facilities, pleasantly landscaped grounds, a small zoo, and—perhaps its greatest attraction— a 3,000 seat theatre where operas were presented throughout the summer months. On the theatre's huge stage a cast of 30 to 50 actors performed nightly versions of *Le Grande Duchess, Said Pasha, Maritana,* and other such pieces.

Still another notable outdoor development was the airdome theatre. The success of park theatres within or beyond city limits illustrated to promoters a public interest in summer theatregoing. If a structure, suitable for summer use, were located in a downtown area, or at least close enough to a city's center of population to eliminate distant travel, would it not have an even greater attractiveness for the public? Since it was to be exclusively a summer operation, functioning no more than twenty weeks a year, large investments in such facilities would be impractical. Thus, the airdome theatre, which could be erected on a vacant lot situated in the main part of a city. The prototype airdome consisted of a covered stage and a seating area open to the sky, all enclosed by a high board fence.

Airdomes came into use sometime after the turn of the century and continued to house summer theatricals until they were forced out of business by street noises from the increasing number of automobiles and by the high values placed on mid-town locations. The first reference to airdomes in the New York *Dramatic Mirror* appeared in 1905 with the listing in the theatrical routings of the Air Dome Theatre in Topeka. Although still regarded in 1907 as "a comparatively new idea in construction," there were "few towns" in the West and Midwest that did not boast of at least one airdome. From Kansas to Texas to Pennsylvania and back again, these poster-adorned, board-fenced summer playhouses could be found in every city and large town. A writer for *Billboard* declared in 1909 that the airdome "has come to stay." The following year another remarked, "While the airdome is still in swaddling clothes, it is safe to predict that within the next ten years it will be as popular as its older sister—the amusement park."

The popularity of outdoor amusements was a welcome prospect for repertoire troupes; for by 1900, repertoire was encountering booking problems with opera house managers. In the first place, the new medium of motion pictures was fast emerging as a strong competitor for opera house time. Secondly, with many opera house managers, the name of repertoire was anathema; primarily because of the widespread practice of play piracy.

Repertoire could not have existed as a low-priced entertainment without play piracy. Managers of repertoire companies had the choice of using the old plays not covered by copyright—but that had been performed to death in all established show territories, of commissioning or writing their own pieces, or of using current hits that demanded high royalty payments. The first choice was the least desirable. Although many troupes retained old favorites in their repertoires, continually altering the titles to disguise the plays' antiquity, the public eventually grew wise to the tactic and demanded something new. To avoid paying for production rights, managers and other members of repertoire troupes became playwrights, re-hashing old plots and devices, re-dressing new and popular pieces, and inventing fresh situations tailored to the special talents of their company. (The practice of using plays written by repertoire people increased as copyright laws became more stringent.) Finally, the most inviting alternative was to use the currently popular pieces, competing with one-night stand companies who held the legitimate rights and who were presenting these new plays at top prices. Since repertoire groups needed an aggregate of at least eight plays, and since they subsisted from admission prices of ten-twenty-thirty cents, it was impossible to pay for new pieces and still operate on a profitable basis. The result was the unauthorized use of most of the currently popular plays.

Play piracy is an age-old vice. Shakespeare suffered the indignity of seeing facsimiles of his works, stolen by former members of his company, published without his consent. And strolling players throughout the intervening years have freely used unauthorized versions of plays which were the properties of the big city playhouses. As a form of protection against this kind of pilfering, play manuscripts were carefully guarded. When a company rehearsed a new piece, each actor received only a portion of it from which to study. These "sides," as they were called, contained the actors' lines and a few words of the preceding ones which served as cues for the actors' speeches.[6]

Piracy reached a peak in the years between 1889 and 1893; at which time the use of unauthorized plays "was rampant in all parts

of the country." But it was especially in the West, claimed the
Dramatic Mirror, that "cheap fly-by-night companies conducted
by irresponsible managers" were most active. Sometimes play titles
were altered to escape detection; other times there was no manner of
attempt to cover up: "The pirates defied the authors to proceed
against them."[7] One manager accused of pirating replied that "in
case Congress sees fit to so amend the statute as to make piracy a
criminal offense, I shall obey it, for I have the greatest respect for
the laws of my country—when the penalty for their violation is jail.
But until that time comes, I take great pleasure in enrolling myself
under the Black Flag."

Managers of local theatres were urged by producing organizations
to close their doors to pirating companies. In 1895, the American
Dramatist Club circulated a list of all copyrighted plays, "leaving no
excuse for any manager who permits a piratical company to enter
his theatre." One writer claims that three-fourths of the local managers were fully aware that these troupes were using unauthorized
manuscripts; but that since first-class companies could not be secured
for their houses, managers were content to bring in hit plays through
the only means available, by engaging repertoire companies that were
pirating these new pieces. Piracy flourished in such western states as
Iowa, Illinois, Indiana, and Wisconsin because of the "liberal patronage"
of the theatregoers and because the old standard plays had been worn
out. When questioned as to why he had booked a particular company
of pirates, one local manager responded lamely that "he had been
hypnotized by the advance agent." Another manager was more frank.
"Why shouldn't we play these companies, bringing a first-class repertoire of New York successes that pack the houses?" he questioned.
"You know what the almighty dollar is, and what runs the house.
They give great satisfaction and have elegant paper which is preferable
to honest companies with 'chestnut' repertoires."

On the other hand, there were many local managers who joined
battle against the pirates by refusing them bookings and by exposing
them through the pages of the *Dramatic Mirror*. The manager of the
Beckwith Memorial Theatre (Dowagiac, Mich.) reported that a McKin-
ley and Wall Company was "the worst I have seen yet." They were
accused of playing *Blue Jeans, The Old Homestead, The Charity Ball,*
and *The Still Alarm,* using three-sheets with Frohman's name listed
as manager. In response to a warning carried in the *Mirror* about a

certain company of pirates, L. L. Tilden, manager of the Atlantic (Iowa) Opera House, wrote:

> Your letter of warning regarding the Rutledge Dramatic Company was duly received. In reply I would say that I had this company booked for my fair date week of September 11. On my request they sent a list of plays they would produce. Among them being your *Blue Jeans* and Thompson's *Old Homestead.* I immediately cancelled them as I have no desire to assist these pirates in their nefarious business. Many others of the same kind know that I will not book them on this account.[8]

Sometimes when the local manager discovered the use of unauthorized pieces only after the company had arrived and was playing in his theatre, he would deduct the amount of royalty from the company's share of the receipts. This happened to the Robert Wayne troupe—a group that advertised themselves as one of the few companies paying royalties for all of their plays—when an amount equal to the royalty for *La Belle Marie* was withheld by the manager of the Chatterton Opera House and duly forwarded to the author.

An example of how a play could get into the hands of pirating managers was cited by Milton Nobles. He stated that no play had been "as extensively and persistently" pirated as his *The Phoenix.* The original pirate was a destitute actor Nobles had hired off the streets of Chicago, who, after being dismissed for incompetency, made a manuscript of the play from memory and sold copies for five and ten dollars each. Since that time (circa 1876), "no repertoire company, large or small, has ever been on the road without having *The Phoenix* as a feature under one title or another." One wily repertoire manager went so far as to step in front of the curtain (to satisfy the local manager) and read a letter allegedly from Nobles that granted him permission to use the play.[9]

The pirates could not have existed in such numbers, however, without agencies that made a business of selling bootlegged manuscripts at nominal fees.[10] Without question, the most notorious of these was Alexander Byers and his Chicago Manuscript Company. Byers' stenographers attended hit plays and copied down the dialogue and stage business. The plays were then mimeographed into manuscripts in Byers' headquarters at 102 So. Halstead St., Chicago, and sold for a fraction of the royalty payments. The 1892 catalogue of the Chicago Manuscript Company read:

In order to avoid unnecessary correspondence, parties ordering plays will please conform to the following rules: Enclose $1 with order for each manuscript. Order will be filled and sent C. O. D. for the balance due with privilege of examination; but will positively not send any manuscript entirely C. O. D.[11]

Byers' company was illicitly selling such plays as *Alabama, A Texas Steer, Blue Jeans, Ole Olson, The Phoenix, The Silver King, Shenandoah, M'liss, Hazel Kirke, The County Fair,* and *Caprice.*

In 1895 Byers issued the following information in a circular:

Hundreds of plays are produced in the country every year, and while the majority of them fail, a few score great successes and make fame and fortune for their authors. The owner of a successful play jealously guards his property, and by every means in his power endeavors to prevent others from obtaining a copy of it. For this reason successful plays are never printed until long after they have ceased to be sources of profit to their producers. And here is where the Chicago Manuscript Company is prepared to be of assistance. This company has been for the past fifteen years in the business of dealing in manuscript plays, supplying to both professional and amateur companies the latest and most popular dramatic successes. In our catalogue can be found almost every play that has met with public approval in this country and England in late years, and we continually add to the list. No matter what style of play you may desire, we are prepared to furnish it at a reasonable price.[12]

Such brazen dealing caused sharp response. "This Byers is a pest to the dramatic profession," one *Mirror* writer proclaimed. "Managers and dramatists should take instant steps to defend the interests of their plays." Another called Byers the most "unblushing and enterprising" of all play thieves in Chicago. And he was denounced in court as "the most notorious play pirate of modern times." Ironically, at the time of this last charge, Byers was in court attempting to prosecute his mimeographer for bootlegging extra copies for personal profit.[13]

Byers was himself no stranger to the courts. In 1898, he was accused of issuing a catalog containing "the names of every play in the English language that is worth a penny" and of offering to sell any six for twenty-five dollars. Byers openly admitted that many of the western managers had obtained plays through the Chicago Manuscript Company. Thereupon, he was taken to court; and federal marshalls confiscated 7,000 assorted manuscripts from the rooms of Byers' establishment. Four years later he was in hot water again when marshalls raided his new headquarters at 144 LaSalle Street, seizing nineteen manuscripts and parts of *You Are a Mason* which had been offered for sale. Still later, when in 1909 a copyright amendment was signed by President Roosevelt, the Managers Association took Byers to court on twenty charges, including sending a stenographer to copy plays, printing plays, and circulating and producing them. In this case, Byers was indicted fifteen times by the federal authorities.

Interestingly enough, within a short time Byers was himself a member of the Managers Association. With his eventual turn to "legitimacy," he continued for many years to be a play broker for tent shows, selling re-writes of popular pieces to managers throughout the Middle West.

Piracy did not stop with the use of unauthorized plays, but extended to the unauthorized use of lithographs in advertising the plays. The advertising paper left behind by the first-class companies was frequently picked up by local billposters and re-sold to the pirating companies. Sam Myers, manager of the William Owen troupe, claimed in 1896 that he had been "besieged" by billposters offering "doctored paper." As proof, Myers submitted the following communication from one of them:

I have on hand 2,000 lithos, ranging from ½-sheet to 3-sheet that are pick-ups, but have been well cared for and are in fairly good shape. I have doctored them so that any company can use them. Will send you 100 samples for $1.00. I think you will be pleased with the stuff when you once see it.[14]

In an attempt to obtain pick-up lithos for *Blue Jeans*, one repertoire manager offered a billposting company in Galesburg, Illinois, three cents apiece. More honest than some in his profession, the billposter turned the letter over to the editor of the *Dramatic Mirror*.

These pick-up lithographs were used effectively by small companies that could not afford to have special paper printed. If the name of a prominent New York producer was included in the advertising, so much the better. One company featuring *Trilby* was said to have used three kinds of paper with A. M. Palmer's name on it. ("They play 10¢ straight and give door prizes to boot.") Otherwise, it was a simple matter for paper to be doctored by a pasted strip across the bottom on which the company name was imprinted along with performance dates.

As could be expected, these rampant copyright abuses led to more stringent legislation of copyright enforcement, making it difficult for pirating companies to operate. A revision of the copyright law that became effective in 1897 was the first of a series of steps aimed at punishment of the guilty. The *Dramatic Mirror*, which had been in the forefront of the battle against pirates since 1881, predicted the revisions would put an end to dishonest play uses, stating, "It will be difficult for those but superficially interested in the new law to realize its importance and the promise of good results to flow from it."

The unprincipled persons who have by various dishonest devices secured copies or semblances of popular plays, in order that they might make illegitimate merchandise of the products of their trickery, will find themselves without occupation, and must go into some other branch of dishonest activity. The small managers whose consciences have permitted them to buy these stolen goods for the purpose of representation, because they knew there was no process that would prevent their use of them, may reform their methods and from this time, perforce, act honestly by confining their operations to plays upon which there is no royalty obligations, or they may make terms with the authors and owners whose rights they have heretofore disregarded; but in either case it will be a long time before they are purged of the odium of willful wrongdoing.15

With the new law "any person publicly performing or representing any dramatic or musical composition shall be liable for damages therefore in a sum not less than one hundred dollars for the first and fifty dollars for every subsequent performance; and, if the unlawful performance or representation be willful and for profit, the guilty person or persons shall be deemed guilty of a misdemeanor, and upon conviction, be imprisoned for a period not exceeding one year."

Under this law, then, the local managers were liable along with traveling managers, actors, and everyone connected with the unauthorized performances. Quite naturally, the opera house managers began to show more concern for honest practices and increased their alertness against unauthorized use of plays. For example, in 1901 the manager of Wilson's Opera House (Beloit, Wisconsin) was said to have "nipped in the bud" an act of piracy in his theatre by his quick action. Hoyt's Stock Company was performing a play called *Pike County People*; mid-way through the evening Wilson discovered it was actually *Way Down East*. He immediately saw to it that the curtain was lowered; and demanded that the company manager make a public explanation and apology. When the manager refused, Wilson promptly cancelled the remainder of the engagement.

There were other pressures, too. One-night stand managers screamed complaints of poor business and blamed it on the repertoire companies, accusing them of controlling the billboards in front of the opera houses where all week their "cheap paper" kept higher priced attractions from using the space. And when companies arrived with high admission prices, the public had just experienced a week of drama selling for ten-twenty-thirty cents and were in no mood to pay more. In a letter to the editor of the *Dramatic Mirror*, Hal Reid called one repertoire group "a worse evil than cheap cotton."

At Houston the Peters Repertoire Company suspended their ten, twenty, and thirty cents entertainment, to allow us to go in at one dollar, following us the next day with the usual matinee. Repertoire companies at ten-twenty-thirty ahead of you, following you, and laying off to let you play![16]

By 1899 it was clear to some local managers that repertoire was killing the one-night stand. To protect his better attractions, E. R. Endly, proprietor of the opera house in Mansfield, Ohio, booked only two repertoire companies a year, one in the spring and one in the fall. Theatre manager John Mishler operated under the policy: "No repertoire companies booked on any terms." He refused, as he described it, to "mislead customers with misrepresentations at cheap prices."

And finally, serving as the last straw for opera house repertoire, the motion picture craze that began in 1896 with the first exhibition of Vitascope at Koster and Bial's Music Hall in New York City had by 1906 reached a degree of public acceptance totally unexpected. Audiences, apparently tired of the phoney realism of melodrama which they had tolerated for so many years, became fascinated by this new medium.

The growth of this new business was exceedingly rapid; nickelodeon theatres appeared in downtown areas almost overnight. The conversion of a store building into a picture theatre was a simple matter. And like the newsreel theatres of later years, it was convenient for shoppers to stop in for the relatively short showings of these early films. Chicago alone had 116 five-cent movie houses by 1907. The following year it was estimated that 20,000 people a day were flocking into New York City nickelodeons. By 1910 some 5,000,000 people daily were attending motion pictures in any one of 12,000 theatres.

Five-cent theatres abound on every hand; their illumination is the most garish, their white and golden fronts are the most inviting, the crowds about them the biggest to be found on the street. Squads of police are necessary in many places to keep in line the expectant throngs awaiting their turn to enter the inner glories.[17]

With such a display of enthusiasm, it was simple to recognize that motion pictures were "driving vaudeville and melodrama out of business." The gallery gods, on whom the live theatres depended, had switched their allegiance to films. By 1910, the "empty store stage" of motion picture development was disappearing; pictures were being shown in such respected New York theatres as the Manhattan, Union Square, Lincoln Square, the Circle, the Majestic, Yorkville, the Savoy, Keith and Proctor's 23rd Street, and the Harlem Opera House. Motion pictures were not only drawing audiences away from the live amusements, they were taking over their facilities as well.

The road was as hard hit as the major cities by the picture craze. One-night stand managers expressed concern in 1907 that film enterprises were "rapidly springing up in hundreds if not thousands of small cities and towns." Touring companies had already suffered the effects of the bicycle and roller skating fads, and were experiencing the inconveniences of the Theatrical Trust; the fear of still another disparagement is understandable. Local theatre managers were succumbing to the opposition by booking films into their houses. Admission prices for cheap melodramas and repertoire companies were ten, twenty, and thirty cents, and for road shows as high as $1.50; motion pictures could be shown for five cents. With the quality of live drama being fed to the provincial houses at its lowest ebb, consisting of tired plays, shoddy scenery and inferior performers, many local managers chose to join the film parade. The remarks of one theatre proprietor in 1907 are indicative of the attitudes of his provincial colleagues.

The picture business is bound to grow because it furnishes satisfying entertainment to the masses at the lowest possible price of admission. There is no use fighting against it. . . . In my opinion the best movement the regular house managers can make is to enter the moving picture field themselves. . . . If I had a theatre in a smaller town playing only two or three attractions a week, with possible dark weeks through failures and cancellations, I would have a moving picture outfit on hand and would run it in my theatre on off days and nights.[18]

Pictures gradually became the exclusive entertainment feature in many of the road theatres, simplifying small town theatre management and eliminating the problems caused by road managers, actors, and unreasonable booking agencies.

Repertoire companies were gradually being squeezed out of many opera houses, making it necessary for them to look beyond the small town theatres to places more remote, where one-night stand companies never appeared, where audiences could not compare entertainment values between ten-twenty-thirty prices and those of a dollar and over, where obscurity was a protection against tightened copyright enforcement, and where operations could be continued throughout the summer months. For some managers looking to improve an increasingly grim situation, the canvas pavilion used by the circus was a promising solution.

CHAPTER IV. DEVELOPMENT OF THE CANVAS THEATRE

THE PRESENT DAY USE OF TENTS FOR SUMMER THEATRICALS WAS popularized by St. John Terrell in 1949. Terrell's canvas pavilion soon proved to be an inexpensive structure in which to produce colorful musical comedy productions while providing a picturesque circus atmosphere for summer theatregoers. Out of this Lambertville (New Jersey) experiment grew a flourishing summer theatre business. Brightly colored domes appeared in all parts of the country, allowing summer impressarios to function in communities that did not already possess adequate theatre facilities. Erroneously hailed by many in 1949 as a theatrical innovation, the tent as a tradition in American theatre dates back more than a century.

The canvas theatre—a simulation of the small town opera house—that came into popular use at the end of the 19th century, evolved from the circus tent. Stage, rigging, chairs and other equipment were placed under the familiar white top and adapted to fulfill needs for portability, designed to be easily erected and taken down and compactly loaded for transporting in the minimum of time and labor.

Although the use of a tent to shelter both actors and audience under a single roof is probably American in origin, canvas or linen covers for theatrical events have been in use for hundreds of years. In the amphitheatre at Pompeii (*circa* 59 A.D.), a Roman wall painting shows a linen canopy which is thought to have been a Campanian invention credited to Quintus Latatius Catulus in about 70 B.C. The awning extended between two towers of the city wall, protecting the ladies' boxes from the direct heat of the sun.

Some manner of English tent is mentioned by Puttenham in his *Arte of English Poesie* published in 1589. In referring to "new comedies or ciuill enterludes," he specifies that such amusements were performed in "open pauillions or tents of linnen cloth or lether, halfe displayed that the people might see." And later, "when Tragidies came vp they deuised to present them vpon scaffoldes or stages of timber, shadowed with linnen or lether as the other." Puttenham explains further that

these stages were made in the forme of a *Semicircle*, whereof the bow serued for the beholders to sit in, and the string or forepart was appointed for the floore or place where the players vttered, and had in it sundrie little diuisions by curteins as trauerses to serue for seuerall roomes where they might repaire vnto & change their garments and come in againe as their speaches & parts were to be renewed.[1]

What appears to be one of the earliest American tents devoted to entertainment was constructed at Chatham Garden, a "resort of beauty and fashion of New York," where proprietor Barriere had been presenting musical programs. In anticipation of dramatic productions for the summer of 1823, the stage and auditorium were remodeled and a "complete Pavilion Theatre" was erected, "the whole covered with a vast expanse of white canvas" designed to "protect the audience from the evening dews."[2] However, there is nothing to suggest that this structure was intended as a portable playhouse; possibly the canvas was held in place by some sort of permanent framework. Further, since Chatham Garden was used for summer gatherings, it is logical to assume that the sides of the pavilion were left open to the cooling breezes.

It was not until the equestrian circuses, previously housed in permanent amphitheatres, took to the road that the tent with canvas top and attached canvas sidewall was evolved. With increased competition among various urban amusements, circus proprietors found city populations insufficient for profitable year around management. When improved roads allowed them to travel with heavily loaded wagons, enterprising showmen trouped their companies down the eastern seaboard and then inland along with the expansion of the frontier. Where halls or barns were not available, shows were performed behind canvas fencing held up by poles, open to the whims of the elements.

We do not know who first used the portable tent to eliminate costly lay-offs caused by rain, but in 1826 the circus of Nathan Howes and Aaron Turner "embarked on a long and successful career under a full top of canvas"; and with this may have begun the history of the modern tent show. The early tents took their shape from permanent equestrian facilities such as Ricketts' Amphitheatre in Philadelphia, a circular building measuring nearly 100 feet across covered by a peaked roof. Thus, tents in the first half of the nineteenth century were round, measuring from 50 to 90 feet in diameter, and held up by a single center pole and several side poles. The Buckley and Weeks Circus, for example, which was organized only a few years after Howes and Turner began touring, used a 75 foot tent that seated some 800 people.

Generally, shows remained small until after the Civil War. With the exception of the ring curbing, Quick and Mead's entire outfit, including the 50 foot top, could be loaded on a two-horse wagon. The distance travelled from one stand to the next averaged fifteen miles. Tents and heavy equipment left the lot each night as soon as they could be struck and loaded to follow the route that had been marked earlier by the "telegraph wagon." Frequently, a fence rail, removed and positioned at a fork or road intersection, indicated the proper direction. When rails were not available, gypsum, flour, or sawdust served as markers. As the caravan neared its destination, the vehicles were halted, cleaned of dust or mud, and, after the workmen had donned their colorful parade costumes, the wagons continued into town as advanced advertising had promised—"The Brilliant Cortege preceded by the Superb Military Band."

Competition pushed circuses to provide greater and greater spectacle and forced them to enlarge their portable facilities. P. T. Barnum, always ready to out-do all competitors, was on the road from 1851 to 1854 (some 20 years after the first recorded circus tent) with his Great Asiatic Caravan, Museum and Menagerie in a tent 110 feet long.

The tent had four center poles; both side poles and center poles were bedecked with various national flags; and the tent entrance was draped with bunting. Although Barnum's tent probably had none, quarter poles placed at intervals between the center and side poles were introduced around this time. As tents increased in width and canvas was made heavier and stronger, this additional support became necessary.

A marked change in the size of circuses and circus equipment appeared in the 1870's. Barnum opened his great Traveling World's Fair in 1871 with "vast tents covering nearly three acres of ground;" and within a few years, the impressario boasted, he had enlarged his "already immense tents three different times" to accommodate the crowds. A second ring and hippodrome track were added about this time by the Great Eastern Show; and by 1885 most of the "big ones" had adopted similar features. With the extra ring the old round top became an oval. Any number of canvas middle pieces could be attached to the round ends to make the tent the desired length, much like adding leaves to a dining room table. The pieces were laced together to be quickly fitted or pulled apart.

The American circus hit the zenith of popularity around the turn of the century. Circus historian Earl Chapin May places the golden era within the years from 1871, when William Cameron Coup "made a first class showman out of P. T. Barnum," to shortly before 1920 when the circus eliminated the time-consuming, bothersome street parade. The Barnum and Bailey combined show moved on ninety double-length railroad cars. Sells Brothers Circus and Menagerie boasted four rings in the big top and fifty-one cages in the menagerie, all transported on forty-five railroad cars. James A. Bailey's street parade was so large and so extravagant that, when the show paraded in Berlin during a European tour, the citizens, thinking that such a spectacle left nothing further to be seen at the performance, returned to their homes without buying tickets to the show. Ringling Brothers' 1893 tent measured 180 by 430 feet and the total tent city required ten acres of land to set up comfortably. Almost every community of five thousand or more could look forward to at least one annual visitation by some attraction laying claim to being the "greatest show on earth." Nearly all men and boys in the United States had seen a circus at least once, the billowing white top being fascinating to all.

The successful use of the tent by American circuses gave rise to other amusements under canvas. Concert and comedy companies, featuring snappy bands and acts of vocal and instrumental virtuousity, adopted this means of barnstorming as early as 1856 when Everett's Varieties' newspaper advertisement invited Opelousas, Louisiana, citizens to "take a seat under Everett's Pavilion." Medicine shows with a frock-coated doctor "sold Kickapoo remedies for a dollar a bottle while minstrel boys played banjos and sang the latest negro melodies." For many years Doc Rucker set up his tent in every likely spot in the South and Middlewest until by 1916 he was wealthy enough to retire to a large ranch in Texas.

Uncle Tom's Cabin companies playing one-night stands under canvas became so numerous that they risked passing each other on the road as one show left town and the next arrived. Writing in 1899, Franklin Fyles states that there were never less than twenty such companies touring—half of them in tents. Actually, many shows trouped the small town circuits unrecognized by historians. Some traveled by wagons from hamlet to hamlet, eating and sleeping under the same stretch of canvas that housed their performances.

The canvas theatre was also used by cultural and religious organizations for theatrical and non-theatrical purposes. In 1842 the Millerites, under the leadership of William Miller (who had set the coming of Christ for April 23, 1843), gathered in large tents carried from city to city by their preachers. Evangelists traveled the "sawdust trail" along the western frontier in gospel tents. As one seasoned pioneer recalled, revival tents and medicine shows were about all that Kansans in those hard years had "to keep their bodies and souls together."

But the most popular use of the tent to shelter cultural events was carried on by Chautauqua in the first quarter of the 20th century. The experiment to use portable theatres in summer Chautauqua circuits began in 1904. The pilot tent was lighted with naphtha lamps hung on the center poles; and the stage and seating were improvised. In 1907 a circuit was formed to include 33 towns in Iowa, Wisconsin, and Nebraska; and within a few years the Chautauqua tent system was on a profitable course.

The brown Chautauqua tents were easily distinguished from the traditional white tops of circuses and other touring theatrical groups. This difference seems hardly accidental. Chautauqua was an institution devoted to programs of education and culture; it appealed to a wide swath of middle class America remote from the urban centers, starved for spiritual excitement, yet devoutly opposed to things theatrical. The white tents of strolling entertainers aroused suspicion in the more puritan minds. Since the church and its auxiliaries—the W.C.T.U., Ladies Aid, Epworth League, and Christian Endeavor—were centers of interest in the social structures of the small towns, scorn of theatrical entertainments was perpetuated through the village churchmen. Therefore, by using brown canvas instead of white, Chautauqua promoters removed any chance of their being identified with "show business"; brown canvas symbolized cultural inspiration—improvement of mind, body and spirit, and after 1912 "the brown tent meant Chautauqua and nothing but."

The interior of the Chautauqua tents more closely resembled a lecture hall than an opera house. Wooden folding benches formed into rows supplied the seating. A small stage or platform at one end of the tent was furnished with a "sylvan backdrop," electric footlights, two chairs, and a table holding a pitcher of ice water and a glass. During the programs, the canvas side walls of the tent were rolled up to take advantage of any breeze that might allow members of the audience to cease their constant fanning. For like the opera house, the Chautauqua pavilion was hot, giving rise to the vaudeville joke, "and under the canvas the heat was intense."

As it was adapted for use as a portable theatre, the tent and its accompanying equipment improved in comfort and transportability. The circus tent was designed for circular seating about a ring or rings; therefore, in making it into a theatre, compromises had to be made. For example, the ends of the circus-style tent were too low to accommodate a stage and stage rigging unless such facilities were brought forward to the first center pole where the canvas peaked to its maximum height. Their positioning placed the center pole at the front of the stage platform and obstructed the view. Nevertheless, for years tent dramatic companies tolerated this nuisance. When, early in his career (circa 1900), veteran showman Horace Murphy suggested to his employer, Doc Rucker, that he find a way to eliminate the pole, Rucker replied, "Well, if you can act in front of that pole you can act behind it. Another thing, if you act behind it, I'm going to pay you."

Many tent managers devised their own arrangement for ridding the stage of the interfering pole. One method was to substitute an A-Frame. The top of the *A* served as the tip of the center pole, holding up the canvas at the stage end of the tent. The *A*'s crossbar, which gave the angled joists support, horizontally spanned the front of the stage above the proscenium opening; and the legs of the *A* below the crossbar stood on each side of the proscenium opening. Thus, the entire lower section of the *A* framed the opening but was masked by a canvas proscenium curtain. In 1905 Baker and Lockwood advertised a variation of the A-Frame principle. Instead of a single center pole in front of the stage, there were two poles, one on either side of the proscenium opening. The poles were clearly visible rising above the proscenium curtain and met in some manner near the peak of the tent to support that end of the canvas. Still another design required taller quarter poles at the stage end. The added elevation allowed the stage to be pushed farther to the rear and away from the first center pole. For this a square or gabled end piece was used instead of the circus-style round end. The Slout Players in Michigan used this method as late as 1927.

The first design for a commercially built dramatic end tent appeared in 1910. In August an illustrated article in *Billboard* announced "something absolutely new in canvas homes for theatrical performance." This "commodious tent especially adapted for theatrical use" was placed on the market by the United States Tent and Awning Company, a Chicago concern. Designed by Walter F. Driver, the commercial name for the tent was Driver's Improved Theatrical Tent. Photographs accompanying the article show both an exterior and interior view. They reveal that this particular model used two center poles and no quarter poles in the area in front of the proscenium. The stage end, or dramatic end, was held aloft by two front stage quarter poles at either side of the proscenium opening and three backstage quarters at the rear of the stage platform. The estimated width of the top is from 40 to 50 feet; anything larger would certainly require the use of quarter poles in the seating area. The obvious purpose of the design was to improve stage viewing by eliminating as many poles as possible.

Still another design for theatrical tents was offered in 1919 by Lou J. Palmer. Not only was the "troublesome center pole" in front of the stage missing, but, the Palmer Stage Top, its originator claimed, equalled the easily manageable round top for riding out bad weather. No explanation was given to show how Palmer's tent differed from Driver's. It is doubtful that it was reproduced commercially, however, since no apparent effort was made to promote its sale.

The especially designed dramatic end tent of 1910 was not extensively used by repertoire shows at this early period. Although many new tent shows were taking to the road, managers preferred to buy used equipment for their initial effort; many could not afford the price of a new tent. Charles Wortham, for example, who first formed his company in 1913, began with a second hand round top, 50 feet wide with a 30 foot middle piece. In 1916 he secured a square end tent from a company in Springfield, Illinois, and rebuilt it to give it a dramatic end. It was not until 1920 that he bought a new Driver's "Special"—a 50 foot top with two middle pieces at a cost of $1,900. In the early 1920's Choate's Comedians was still using a large circus tent that "covered a city block." The outfit had five center poles, one of which stood directly in front of the stage.

Another reason managers may have rejected the dramatic end design is that it restricted the size of the canvas spread. With no supporting pole mid-way along the proscenium line a water pocket, destructive to the canvas, was apt to form in heavy rainstorms. In later designs a grommet hole was placed at the point of danger to accommodate a supplementary pole which would eliminate the formation of water pockets during a storm. Still, the width of the tents was limited to between fifty to sixty feet. The large shows needed the seating space that tents up to seventy feet furnished. For the advantage of a large tent, managers of the bigger companies preferred either to rig their own devices for eliminating the pole in front of the stage or suffer its presence.

Yet another design, perhaps unrelated to our story, but interesting as a means of comparison, was put forth by the Moreau Brothers of France in 1911. A canvas theatre was planned for Firmin Gemier, director of the Theatre Antoine in Paris, to take his company on a tour of the provinces. M. Gemier's need for a portable playhouse was not unlike the needs of American managers.

He was discouraged on finding everywhere the same commonplace municipal theatre, with its dusty and worn velvet chairs, its inadequate stage facilities, scanty scenery, and, at the end of the performances, the local treasurer demanding from 40 to 70 per cent of the receipts in return for the miserable accommodations.[3]

The plan was to utilize two tents, each 246 feet long and 131 feet wide, spacious enough to accommodate three thousand people. While one outfit was being used for performances at one location, the other was to be dismantled and erected at another. Gemier's tent was a departure from the American dramatic end design. For one thing, no poles interfered with the audience's view of the stage; the canvas was hung from an elaborate steel frame. Five girders, each 56 feet high, with large flat bases for placement on any stretch of level ground were connected at the top with a transverse girder spanning 90 feet. The entire framework was assembled in a horizontal position and then hoisted vertically by a steam tractor used to transport the equipment. The steel pieces were constructed to be unbolted and packed in short lengths for shipment.

The interior resembled the interior of a theatre. An elaborate proscenium wall separated the front and backstage areas. The stage, mounted on trestles, was equipped to allow scenery to be rolled on and off by means of hand winches. In front of the proscenium, a floor was inclined to the rear of the house, making a "sufficient slope for the stage to be clearly visible to every person" in the huge tent. The seating consisted of cane benches, orchestra boxes formed by three rows of folding armchairs, and private boxes placed on two specially constructed trailers. The entire floor of the theatre was carpeted and the doors were hung with lush draperies, justifying Gemier's claim that his tent theatre was "equal to the most luxurious in Paris."

Clearly, a portable theatre such as Gemier's would have been impractical for American managers whose tent shows required maximum portability at minimum cost. The heavy equipment took too long to assemble and dismantle; tent theatres in this country had to be torn down, transported, and set up without the loss of a day's performance. To make use of two complete outfits as Gemier did would have been out of the question with managers in the business of making money from surprisingly low admission prices.

American repertoire managers who framed their shows too elaborately often found themselves in financial difficulty. Texas manager Charles Harrison had a passion for large outfits. Shortly before World War II his show was so heavy it took a day to tear down and three days to set up. He was forced to play two-week stands in the larger cities; even so, only ten nights of the two weeks were left for performances. His huge tent accommodated some 3,000 people. Regular opera seats were fastened in place on an inclined wooden flooring. Opera boxes were used near the stage on both sides of the house. Dressing rooms were portable booths built to service two actors each. The large stage

– 43 –

was dressed with an impressive array of heavy scenery. But Harrison was continually "going broke" from this oversized outfit. Neil Schaffner, a highly successful tent showman in his own right, recalls that Harrison kept a smaller unit in storage that he would alternately take on the road to "get well" enough to go back to the larger one.

Managers like Harrison took pride in their tents and were constantly adding new twists and innovations. In the 1920's when competition among shows was intense, the Paul English company touring Louisiana carried a rising orchestra pit. A hole was dug in front of the stage in each town and from it a large orchestra was slowly lifted into view at the opening of each night's program. The show also boasted an ornate water fountain displayed by colored lights, located at the entrance of the tent. One season, Harley Sadler, who operated a show in Texas, used a tent designed with a fly loft over the stage, allowing for scenery to be raised out of sight as in the permanent theatre buildings.

Although there was variation in size and cost of equipment, the basic lay-out for all tent theatres was similar. There were special entrance facilities, both reserved and general admission seating, a stage with stage rigging and scenery, and normal backstage conveniences. The entrance, designated by a canvas canopy or marquee, served as a flashy facade to enhance the tent's appearance as well as a functional theatre lobby where tickets were sold from a "high box" and where "bally boards" displayed pictures of the acting company. Seating space within the tent was divided into separate areas for bleachers and folding chairs. Bleachers, called "blues" from the blue flat-board seating of the circus, were general admission seats designed for easy assembly and compact loading. Boards ten to twelve feet in length were placed over stringers and held erect by wooden jacks; rope lacing kept everything firmly in position. To add stability, a stake or "toe pin" was driven at the base of each stringer. Still, on sandy or filled lots there was always the danger of the seats falling apart while loaded with spectators.[4] Reserved seats, for which a higher admission was charged, were separated from the "blues" by a canvas fence. Any number from two hundred to a thousand folding chairs or benches were placed in rows with the customary double aisles. Tickets for these seats were sold inside the tent at the entrance to the section, from where the seller might chant, "Nice, comfortable high-back chairs, down where you can see and enjoy the show!"

Occasionally, the large tent outfits were equipped with wooden flooring that either increased in elevation toward the rear of the tent, allowing for better viewing, or just raised the seating off the damp ground. Copeland Brothers Stock Company reported as early as 1908 that they were "equipped like a first-class theatre," even using "portable opera chairs." And eight years later Crawford's Comedians announced that their reserved seats were "elevated from the ground, keeping them dry and comfortable," a feature that was new to the company. It is doubtful that tent flooring was used extensively; such a feature was cumbersome and seems hardly to have been worth the effort.

In an attempt to simulate opera house construction even further, some of the large tent shows included opera boxes. These exclusive seats with plush furnishings and brass railings were located near the stage on both sides of the auditorium. The huge tent of the Guy E. Long's Associated Players (90 feet wide and 190 feet long) was equipped in 1920 with 250 such seats raised off the ground and covered with white canvas. But in most shows, boxes were not used. Even in Texas where show outfits tended to be larger than usual they were said to have been a "rare thing."

The stage and stage service area was designed to accommodate the traditional theatrical necessities. Backstage activity was screened by a curtain that hung the full width of the tent. This canvas proscenium had the customary picture-frame opening behind which was rigged a front curtain as well as a "specialty" or "olio" curtain used for the entr'acte entertainment. A wooden framework was suspended above the stage proper from which scenery could be hung. The area behind the stage was reserved for dressing rooms and storage. Usually there were only two dressing rooms, one each for men and women, placed on ground level at either side of the stage and curtained off for privacy. However, some managers found it advantageous to use dressing room trailers or vans that were driven into place along-side the stage; this allowed the actor to dress at stage level and eliminated loading and unloading heavy wardrobe trunks.

The remainder of backstage area was utilized for scene storage. The better tent companies dressed their stages as elaborately as comparable house shows of the period, with ceiling pieces, practical doors and windows, flat scenery, and appropriate furniture. Horace Murphy, for example, toured his California territory in 1916 with 180 flats and 28 drop curtains. This sizeable inventory required a large storage space free from the danger of water damage. Some shows eliminated the space problem by using tie-on Diamond Dye scenery, cyclorama sets of canvas with details painted in dye. Such pieces were held in place by strings tied to the stage framework at the top; after being pulled taut, they were tacked at the bottom to the stage flooring. The die did not run if the scenery became wet; and the canvas could be easily folded and stored compactly in trunks.

The stage platform was designed for portability. The usual assembly consisted of flatboards placed across two-by-six stringers held up by wooden jacks. Some managers used truck or trailer beds equipped with sides that let down to form an expanse of floor. Either way, a stage could be constructed within an hour's time. Sizes varied with the size of the canvas theatre. In 1924, the J. Doug Morgan Stock Company carried a stage measuring 34 feet wide by 14 feet deep that fitted into a tent 70 feet wide.

The methods of theatre lighting closely followed those used by the circus. From the primitive candle chandeliers of the first part of the 19th century, improvements led to gas and finally to electricity. W. L. Wilson reported in 1912 that at that time tent theatres were using three forms of illumination: 1) the kerosene pressure system, "perfected to a high degree," and used by a majority of the companies; 2) the calcium carbon light or acetylene gas light; 3) and the electric light. Electricity came into use for tent theatres shortly after 1900. As early as 1870 Cooper and Bailey featured electric lights in their circus tent and claimed the exclusive right to display such equipment. Ringling Brothers Circus began experimenting with electrical power in 1903; but the following year the show returned to gaslight, using the Bolte and Weyer system. Gas, placed in tanks at the base of each center pole, was forced by compressed air to generators where it was vaporized and then delivered by pressure to chandeliers of 60 Welsbach mantle lamps. It wasn't until 1909 that the Ringling show made full use of electric lights. Tent dramatic companies followed this same pattern. Minnelli Brothers Stock Company carried an electric light plant as early as 1905; while that same year Sterling Dramatic Company was still equipped with "the new gas light." Shows could either hook up to city electric power or carry their own generators. The former was said to have been "so poor that it is almost worse than nothing" in those early years; but as municipal facilities improved, most of the tent shows made use of them.

With the addition of electricity, the tent completed its evolution from circus round top to canvas opera house. The simulation was as complete as portability allowed. The large tents could accommodate more spectators than the small town theatres, and at the same time offer audiences seating that was just as commodious and stage facilities that were every bit as functional. And above all, the tent show proprietor did not have to split box office receipts with local managers. The tent and its theatrical equipment, developed for portability and low cost operation, did not change in form to any extent after the dramatic end came into popular use. By 1920 the mold was set.

CHAPTER V. THE EMERGENCE OF TENT REPERTOIRE

DRAMA AND ACCOMPANYING SPECTACLE WAS AN IMPORTANT PART
of circus programming for many years. As early as 1795 Ricketts'
Amphitheatre in New York was thoroughly renovated to include
"scenery, machinery, decorations, etc., incident to stage performance," a move that marked the combining of the equestrian arena
and the dramatic stage into a single spectacle and set the pattern
for future circus programming. Dramas involving horsemanship
were of particular interest to the circus which at that time was
primarily an equestrian entertainment. Early 19th century extravaganzas such as *Timour the Tartar* and *The Cataract of the Ganges*
were adapted for use in the ring, forcing equestrian performers to
become actors and, according to Odell, "in some cases, very good
ones." When the circus began performing out-of-doors the traditional use of drama within its programs remained; deep-rooted
elements such as tableaux, ballet, minstrelsy, and grand pageantry
were continually utilized. As late as the end of the 19th century
Ringling Brothers Circus was using scenery and effects on a platform at one of the huge tent. Under the canvas cover, the stage
appeared alongside the ring as standard circus equipment.

One of the earliest presentations of drama under canvas occurred
at Rock Island, Illinois, in Robinson's Athenaeum, under the manage-

ment of Yankee Robinson. Fayette Lodawick Robinson, a one-time cobbler, dancing teacher, and exhibitor of religious paintings, began his acting career in 1835 as Jonathan Doolittle in *A Yankee in England,* a role from which he presumably took the name "Yankee." Robinson claims to have made a tent with his own hands in 1851, while wintering in Rock Island, Illinois. Using the tent in summer and halls in the winter, Robinson and his troupe toured the Middlewest, performing such pieces as *Lady of Lyons, The Seven Clerks, Idiot Witness, Uncle Tom's Cabin,* and *A Secret.* Gradually, circus acts were added to the dramatic entertainment until, by 1857, Robinson was the proprietor of the Yankee Robinson Circus, which toured successfully for many years.[1]

Reference to tent touring companies is rare before 1885. If the recollection of John S. Richardson is correct, the Wright and O'Hara's Pavilion Dramatic Company was performing one-night stands of *The Hidden Hand* in New York State around 1863. The outfit traveled by old fashioned packet boat, performing in towns along the Seneca Canal. Then, in February of 1885, A. L. Wilbur announced plans in the New York *Dramatic Mirror* for a summer operation that was to "compete with the circuses." His scheme called for a twenty-week season of one-week stands under canvas to begin in Meriden, Conn., in a tent large enough to hold 4,000 spectators. And the following year the *Dramatic Mirror* observed that the use of a tent for entertainment purposes was "no longer confined to the circus," for such amusements as opera, vaudeville, and minstrelsy were being presented in canvas theatres. Furthermore, it was "only in the past few years" that tents had "begun to dot the landscape in such great numbers." This activity led to the prediction that "summer entertainments under canvas will become an institution."[2]

Most provincial theatres were dark throughout the summer months, for audiences refused to attend summer entertainments in buildings with no means of proper ventilation. Thus, local managers were forced to close their doors during the hot weather and occupy themselves with refurbishing and booking attractions for the winter season. Rather than disband in the spring, repertoire companies chose to function year-round, using a tent for the summer months. The sidewalls could be raised or opened out in the hottest of weather to get the benefit of the cooling night air. And, in addition, such a theatre could be taken into communities where untapped audiences were eager for the novelty of dramatic performances. Thus, early repertoire organizations such as the Harry Shannon Stock Company, Angell's Comedians, Hunt Stock Company, and Maxam and Sights could operate under canvas for approximately twenty weeks and then move back into houses when the weather turned severe.

Although tent shows were modeled after opera house repertoire, not all tent managers were trained in the repertoire system; some began their touring with variety companies. John W. Ginnivan took his vaudeville show under canvas in 1870 and toured for some ten years until he organized a dramatic company and played three-night stands with a repertoire of *Faust, The Flying Dutchman,* and *The Haunted Man.* The Ginnivan name became synonymous with tent repertoire for summer audiences in Ohio and Michigan and was perpetuated when a son and daughter each organized a company—the Frank Ginnivan Stock Company and the Norma Ginnivan Stock Company—and enjoyed many years of successful operation. Roy E. Fox, owner of the Roy E. Fox's Popular Players, who boasted, in 1917, a record seventeen years without closing, began his tent management with the Lone Star Minstrels. Jethro Almond operated a vaudeville and picture show until, following World War I, the show was re-organized to feature dramatic offerings, and continued to tour in this manner through the summer of 1929. The Winninger Brothers started as a family orchestra under the direction of their mother. After performing in vaudeville and briefly in the circus, the boys formed a repertoire company with Frank, John, Charles (who went on to star in motion pictures), Adolphe, and Joe, all participating in the management.

In the years prior to 1900 tent repertoire companies toured in relative obscurity, performing the same plays as the house organizations of the time. A week's repertoire might have included *Jack Sheppard, East Lynne, The Hidden Hand, Fanchon the Cricket, Lady Audley's Secret, Hazel Kirke, The Two Orphans, Kathleen Mavourneen,* and *Camille.* Each play was spiced with assorted specialties placed between the regular acts of the drama—singing, dancing, recitations, instrumental numbers, and comedy patter. The companies made short jumps from one small town to the next, generally remaining in each place three days to a week, operating within a limited territory to which the troupes returned year after year.

Recollections of tent show people establish the managers who pioneered. J. N. Rentfrow, said to have "entered the game" in the early 1870's, was touring Rentfrow's Jolly Pathfinders through a Texas territory by 1880. The Wilbur M. Williams Dramatic Company was another early entry. Tent show manager Earl Hawk has stated that in 1881 when Williams, playing week stands in the West, found indoor accommodations too small to handle the crowds, he purchased a tent; but continuous rainstorms forced him to place it in storage. Remembering differently, another reporter recalls that after playing under canvas for three towns, Williams' company encountered "one of those old time sand storms" and there wasn't enough left of the tent to "make a set piece." Another Williams, unrelated, came to America from England in 1882, organized the Williams Stock Company and toured throughout the southeastern part of the country. Eventually, Tom and Fannie Williams raised a family of ten performing children—Ina, Fannie, Marie, Ona, Katie, May Blossom, Tom, Joe, Al, and Johnny. As the children married and left the company they formed other tent repertoire troupes— the Ina and Billy Lehr Company, Mason-Williams (Dick and Fannie) Company, Johnny J. and Betty Williams Company, Robert and Ona Demorest Company, Harry and Katie Keene Company, Marie De-Gafferelly Company, Joe Williams Company, Tom Williams Company, Al Williams Company, and Elmer and Marie Lazone's Original Williams Stock Company.[3]

It was not until the turn of the century, however, that repertoire under canvas grew sufficiently to attract attention. Just how many shows were touring during the period from 1900 to 1910 is impossible to ascertain; certainly there were well over one hundred. Although companies operated in every part of the country, the greatest concentration at this time seems to have been in the Middlewest and South. No significant changes in operation appeared until the following decade; perhaps because of the lack of communication between managements. Although *Billboard* began carrying a news column with the heading "Dramatic" around 1904, few shows took advantage of it to relate their activities. Most preferred to operate in obscurity, allowing successes and failures to go unrecorded. It was not until 1914 that a full page was devoted to tent repertoire, a move that established the weekly *Billboard* as the tent showman's Bible and created an awareness of industry activity among tent show personnel.[4]

The repertoire tent show was basically a rural theatre and, as such, was influenced by the attitudes of the agrarian class and by agricultural economy. It is crucial in following the development of tent repertoire to keep this clearly in mind.

From the broad view, agriculture was in decline during the time tent shows developed and prospered. Beginning in the latter half of the 19th century and continuing to the present, the farmer has gradually lost his political, social and economic power. The early 1890's were the blackest years the farmer had ever experienced. No longer the self-sufficient yeoman of yesteryear, the farmer of the nineties was a businessman subject to market fluctuation, inconsistencies in transportation costs, and to the necessities for expansion and mechanization. He felt the abuses of high interest rates, over-production, and increased costs of commodities. Further, he found himself caught in the pinch of over-speculation in farm land. In Kansas and North Dakota there was a mortgage for every two persons; in Nebraska, South Dakota, and Minnesota, one for every three. At the same time, agrarian population was declining. In 1880 about one-fifth of the country's population lived in cities of 8,000 or more; by 1900 the percentage had increased to one-third. Farm youth, disenchanted with rural life and enticed by the wages of industry and the exciting pulse of the city, were leaving their homesteads. And finally, with increased means of transportation and communication, farm isolation was diminished, a condition that was at first a threat to the farmer's traditional way of life.

It would seem paradoxical that a theatre dependent on agriculture would blossom into being at the very time when agriculture was losing ground; but during the infant years of tent repertoire—the turn-of-the-century years—the farmer was experiencing a temporary prosperity that was to last longer than in any other peacetime period. Agriculture began an improved state of health by 1897 when it was reported that "every barn in Kansas and Nebraska has had a new coat of paint." There was a rise in farm prices, a reduction in freight rates for farm products, and an increased export market. Wheat rose from 72 cents a bushel in 1896 to 98 cents in 1909; corn prices increased from 21 cents to 57 cents, and cotton from 6 to 14 cents a pound.

During two decades of farm prosperity, the repertoire tent show developed into a rural theatrical institution. Without a receptive farm market to encourage growth and development, the repertoire companies would have expired as a theatrical form along with the opera house and the one-night stand.

The early tent shows experienced hostility from small town inhabitants, stemming in part from fly-by-night circuses and medicine shows. With the adoption of tents for traveling Chautauqua and with the inclusion of dramas within the cultural Chautauqua programs, tents began to lose the stigma of iniquity, and small town prejudice improved toward the theatre in general. Before the small town mind was opened, traveling companies resorted to the same kind of semantical trickery as the local theatre managers did when they called their establishments *opera houses* and *academies of music.* Such duplicity was used by the 19th century circuses to sell a gullible public on the "spiritual and educational" values in circus entertainments. Bandwagons were ornamented with scenes from mythology and Biblical history. Pageants were performed in the ring utilizing themes from religious and historical antiquity, garishly costumed with alleged authenticity. With the merging of circus and menagerie, a move purposely brought about to give the circus respectability, zoological references were added to advertising. A public interested in learning about natural history was shown animals with names conveniently concocted to excite attendance— a white-tailed gnu was once called a "horned horse." The most useful quality of a circus press agent became his sesquipedalian dexterity in adequately extolling the "Scintillating, Kaleidoscopic, Unparalleled, Heterogeneous Aggregation of Multiplied Wonders" as something to enlighten and inspire both young and old.

The touring *Uncle Tom's Cabin* companies, too, made use of educational and religious motifs in their advertising. A flier of the 1890's read, "The most exacting Christian people never hesitate to visit this great Moral show."[5] Another advertisement promised "The Grandest Production ever given of Harriet Beecher Stowe's immortal work, read and admired all over the world, and by the *Clergy* and *Christian People of all Creeds.*" To assist in public education, shows offered such added features as the "First Presentation on any Stage of a GENUINE COTTON GIN AND PRESS IN FULL OPERATION."

Moral and educational spectacle within the play was emphasized by scenic tableaux portraying "Eva in heaven and the beautiful gates ajar," and "The historic slave market and many other scenes that go to form a great production in this grand old historical play." One-night stand attractions could misrepresent in this manner; they arrived in a town one morning and were gone before the following sun-up. But for repertoire companies that remained in one spot for a week, outlandish claims had to be minimized. The productions were the proof of respectability; and so the plays took on the character of small town morality.

The influence of Chautauqua on rural America cannot be over-estimated. For the small communities Chautauqua Week was the event of the year. Many families camped out for the entire series of programs. Those who lived near enough to commute packed lunches of fried chicken which they ate from their "rigs" parked in the shade of a tree. In 1912 there were more than one thousand independent Chautauquas in the United States, averaging ten-day sessions each to an audience of about one thousand people per day. By 1920, an estimated ten and a half million attended 8,500 Chautauquas. And by the peak year of 1924, over thirty million Americans in some twelve thousand rural communities crowded into the brown tents. An historian of the period recounts:

No American institution is more typical than the traveling Chautauqua which has had such a mushroom of growth among our small towns in the past few years. Nothing more illustrates the mental poverty of Main Street than the eagerness with which our millions grasp at even so much opportunity for broadening horizons as its average program affords. From its scope and direction you may learn of the national hunger for self-improvement, information, advancement; and by the rigid censorship on things said from its platform is strikingly illustrated the limitations the typical American imposes on himself and others.[6]

Themes from the Chautauqua programs were often referred to as "mother, home and heaven." A good deal of care was taken by local sponsors and by platform entertainers to make the programs spiritually invigorating, morally instructive, and highly educational, in conformance with rural definitions of spirituality, morality, and education. Therefore, at the outset, traveling (or tented) Chautauquas were reluctant to include the drama.

The small town audiences demanded the escape from their daily lives that drama affords, but without the taint of greasepaint and scenery and other theatrical accessories that were associated with evil. Chautauqua satisfied this demand, prior to the introduction of plays, through dramatic readings, impersonations, and acts featuring rapid changes of character. Although Chautauqua programs were performed in a tent, on a stage, by professional entertainers, for which admission was charged, extreme care was taken to keep this separate from "show business." The performing artists, many of them professional actors filling out an otherwise summer lay-off, were called "entertainers," "readers," "elocutionists," "impersonators," and "quick change artists." William Sterling Battis impersonated a gallery of Dickens' characters. Benjamin Chapin read dramatic monologues of Lincoln. Frederick Warde and Leland Powers and Katherine Ridgeway were the Shakespearean people. Charles Rose Taggart gave impressions of "down east" characters. Montaville Flowers devoted an entire evening to *Ben Hur*, playing all the parts "except the horses."[7]

The use of plays, presented unashamedly as plays, was a gradual addition to the Chautauqua platform. Willis Watson Ginn became famous for enacting a complete drama, impersonating each character himself, changing his costume, his walk, his gestures, and his voice. And Mrs. M. C. Hutchinson offered a one-woman show with a repertoire of such plays as *What Every Woman Knows, The Importance of Being Ernest,* and *Rebecca of Sunnybrook Farm,*"changing her voice, making love to herself, responding, breaking in as a great blustering villain, resuming as a mild shrinking maid, creating and maintaining the illusion to the last curtain."[8] Then, in 1913, the daring step was taken. The Ben Greet Players that had been touring the United States presenting Shakespeare, for the most part out-of-doors, was contracted to perform *Comedy of Errors.* The play was scoured of any lines or words that might offend the fan-wielding midwesterner and presented on a comparatively bare stage in front of a plain backdrop. Shakespeare was an instant hit on the Chautauqua circuits. And with this, more dramatic activity followed: a two-people dramatization of *Shore Acres* by Charles and Lois Craig, Claire Vaughan Wales and a company of six in *Rejuvenation*, and the Moroni Olsen Players and the Cambridge Players, all serving to popularize and legitimize the drama for the small town audience. Softened by the cultural sledge hammer of Shakespeare, audiences were ready and willing to accept plays of more frivolous character. Following the cautious offering of *The Servant in the House* came *The Melting Pot, It Pays to Advertise, Nothing but the Truth, Turn to the Right, Lightnin',* and *Peg O' My Heart,* until by 1924 the most popular feature in Chautauqua was the drama.

It is reasonable to assume that the acceptance of drama by the small town Chautauqua audiences had a dampening effect on the formerly bristling antagonisms toward actors and everything theatrical. Certainly Chautauqua Week in the various communities was supervised by the most conservative local people, the clergy, the bankers, the women's organizations; their acceptance of drama as part of a Chautauqua program was an indication to those in the community who looked to them for moral leadership that perhaps the theatre was not as dangerous as had been believed. Actors were allowed on the Chautauqua platform and were boarded overnight in local homes. Costumes and make-up, constituting what was formerly thought of as deceitful impropriety, were used freely. And the dramas, most of which could no longer be classed as culture, many being out and out comedies, were not only accepted but promoted. The most skeptical could not help but be comforted by the knowledge that "this was Chautauqua—the lofty of principle —the well-sponsored—and by the fact that the minister on the bench at the right, and the deacon's wife up front, who had also bought season tickets, were laughing as heartily as the unwashed flock."9

The pulpit and the stage that were interchangeable on the Chautauqua platform became exchangeable on the community level. In 1921 evangelist Billy Sunday spoke from the stage of O'Keefe and Davis' tent, thanking the management for allowing him a rostrum and expressing a kindly feeling "toward theatrical folk in general." The same year Ira Jack Martin, a member of the Stanton-Huntington Players, was invited to preach a sermon at the Christian Church in Beallsville, Ohio, the church being without a regular minister. The congregation for the affair was said to have been one of the largest in years. And following the "very interesting and convincing sermon," the townspeople extended an invitation to the show and its personnel to play in their town again. The following year, during an engagement in northern Indiana, the Frank Ginnivan Stock Company was honored when a local minister, after asking for permission to address the audience from the stage, complimented Mr. Ginnivan and the troupe on the quality of the show and the conduct of the company. This kind of reaction from community leaders indicates that repertoire tent shows were finally not only accepted but respected as well.

It is almost unbelievable that someone as remote from rural America as Sarah Bernhardt could have influenced the growth of provincial tent shows; but in all probability this was the case. When Bernhardt found many theatres closed to her during her 1905-06 tour of the United States, she was forced to create makeshift arrangements. On tour in Texas, where theatre managers were particularly hostile toward her, her agents purchased a circus tent and substituted it where indoor facilities could not be obtained. The attendant publicity, with the most exciting and well-known actress of the age showing a willingness to perform in a tent, served to dignify the use of the canvas theatre.

The tour caused resentment from the outset. In the first place, theatre managers felt that Bernhardt's terms were too demanding, for they exceeded the customary house split. Her agent had lured her to America with the offer of $1,000 a performance, plus fifty percent of the nightly gross receipts if they were over $4,000, and weekly hotel expenses of $200. Secondly, competing road companies feared the magic of the Bernhardt name which brought "hundreds of inhabitants from small out-of-way places, who streamed into the big towns to see 'the Bernhardt'," and who spent their money in holiday fashion to the loss of the shows that followed in her wake. Wise house managers knew that one night's boxoffice from a Bernhardt appearance would not compensate for the loss of bookings caused by disgruntled touring companies. And, lastly, Bernhardt was caught in a power play between the Shuberts, who booked her tour, and the Theatrical Syndicate.

The Syndicate was a formidable foe of the French star. Organized in 1896 to cope with theatrical instability caused by the panic of 1893, the Syndicate controlled a majority of the theatres in the United States. But monopolistic practices had aroused indignation from a sizable part of the theatrical world and from the American public. When Bernhardt herself had been associated with the Syndicate in 1901, she denounced it as "a direct menace to the drama destroying personal freedom of action without which art cannot exist."[10]

By 1905 the Syndicate had recognized in the Shuberts a competitor that was beginning to be troublesome. The Shubert brothers had accumulated nearly thirty major theatres and gave every indication of a continued growth; so the Syndicate set about to crush its adversary before it became too large to deal with. Shubert-managed artists found Syndicate houses closed to them. The theatres of the western states, far from Shubert strength and solidly behind the Syndicate, were the most impenetrable for independent attractions. The situation was best exemplified in Texas where the powerful Greenwall circuit booked only Syndicate talent, and where it was generally known "that the Trust absolutely controls the theatres in the leading cities."[11] Because of this monopoly, bookers were sending out inferior companies to the extent that Texans "felt the results of Trust neglect harder than theatre-goers in other states."[12]

When Bernhardt arrived in New York on the French liner *La Touraine* on November 18, 1905, she must have anticipated the difficulty she was to encounter in securing theatres. But Bernhardt had a penchant for colorful publicity; and squaring off against the powerful Syndicate was certain to result in an enormous amount of newspaper attention. So the brash, new Shubert booking agency, at the time engaged in a battle with the Syndicate, was ideal to assist her personal manager, William F. Conner, in arranging the tour. What is more, Bernhardt headed straight into the Texas stronghold of the Syndicate in March of 1906, where public and press were only too willing to react against past monopolistic practices and support sympathetically a fight for open theatres. With a star of Bernhardt's stature, the call to the colors was an easy matter.

Just how the plan to perform under canvas originated is not clear. A Bernhardt biographer has stated that the French actress "suggested to her impresario" the possible use of a tent.[13] On the other hand, an account by Conner, "her impresario," implies it was his scheme, since in his judgment it was the "only solution" to the Syndicate blockade. Whoever was the author of the idea, the canvas theatre provided an answer to the dilemma; and, in addition, it enriched publicity opportunities while furnishing far greater seating accommodations than Bernhardt could have found in the permanent theatres that were closed to her.

As must have been expected, Madame Bernhardt's announcement that she would be performing in a tent created a stir of indignation. Actor Richard Mansfield, representing the professional point of view, wrote the Syndicate booking office that

the policy of the theatre should be to give the public the best regardless of
party feeling. . . . For Madame Bernhardt to play nightly in a tent would
be to endanger her health, and the responsibility would be lodged at your
door, and America would be blamed as inhospitable.[14]

The Houston *Post*, expressing a universal feeling of vexation, termed
the barring of Bernhardt from Texas theatres "an outrage that effects
not only the world's most distinguished living actress, but the art loving people of Texas who desire to witness her plays." The blame for
this indignity was placed directly on the "contemptible spirit of the
Syndicate to punish Madame Bernhardt because she does not submit
to its domination." Further, the *Post* charged that in such a policy
"the rights of the public" were "ruthlessly ignored and the laws of
the state contemptuously violated by these theatrical leeches." An
invitation was put forward by Attorney General Davidson of Texas
to investigate the matter as it affected anti-trust violation. These
quotes, reprinted in the *Dramatic Mirror*, indicate the support offered
Bernhardt by the press wherever she appeared.
  The Syndicate and its associates denied all charges. In reply to
Mansfield, the bookers claimed that Bernhardt had not applied to
them for any dates because her managers (referring to the Shuberts)
had "a circuit of theatres of their own;" further, they scoffed at the
danger and necessity of her playing in a tent. In Texas, the Greenwalls,
insisting that their theatres were not closed to the French star, refused
to admit they had any connection with the Syndicate.
  Amid this agitation the Bernhardt tent was erected in Cycle Park,
situated in a suburban area three miles from Dallas and connected to
the city by trolley line. Conner had gone to Texas in order to personally
"supervise the making of the tent." And Madame Bernhardt, relishing
the adventure, offered many suggestions for the design of what she
called her "canvas temple." When she arrived in Dallas on the night
before opening, her first words to Conner were, "Where is my tent?"[15]
  The tent was the typical white top of the circus, held aloft
by two center poles and several quarter poles. Inside, however,
a sounding board was hung over the large stage to improve the
acoustics. The use of tall quarter poles at the stage end of the
tent allowed the stage platform to be located farther toward the

rear, eliminating the sight obstructing pole at the front stage line. For seating, long benches, capable of holding five or six spectators each, filled the huge auditorium. Finally, by furnishing the news media with a press gallery which included telegraph and cable facilities, Bernhardt arranged that her venture not go unnoticed.

She could not have hoped for a greater reception than she received in Dallas. The public response represented "as much a popular demonstration of the citizens of Texas against the arbitrary action of the Theatrical Trust in barring the great actress from all the playhouses of the state as an appreciation of Bernhardt's art."[16] The success of the evening was impressive. The intended publicity was achieved, and the tempest over Syndicate behavior provoked public indignation and press response. Bernhardt had indeed scored her points.

With such success at the outset, the tent was no longer needed for publicity. Thus, as far as it can be determined, Bernhardt's canvas tour of the West ended at her next stop—Waco. The company used the Hancock Opera House in Austin (March 28), Beethoven Hall in San Antonio (March 29), and the Grand Theatre in Tyler (April 2).

Aside from achieving the desired publicity, there were other factors that led to Bernhardt's abandoning the tent. The rainy weather she encountered during her limited tenting experience may have demonstrated the disadvantages of her "canvas temple." A wet tent is heavy to move. And rain beating down on tight canvas creates a tumult of sound overpowering to even the strongest pair of male lungs. Damp dressing rooms and muddy lots are an extreme discomfort to someone used to performing in the first-class theatres of the world. And lastly, even a dry tent is a problem to move and erect, particularly when a company is involved in one-night stands. Veteran showman, Ted North, summed things up simply: "They found out they had too many problems in moving the tent."[17]

Bernhardt achieved additional publicity when she offered her tent for a Chicago benefit performance for the sufferers of the San Francisco earthquake. A tent was needed because, in her words, there was "no theatre in Chicago large enough to accommodate all the people who will want to witness the performance."[18] The attention given the planning of the benefit is indicated by a *Billboard* prediction that it would be "the greatest theatrical benefit performance ever given in the history of the stage."

The program included a cross section of the Chicago theatrical crafts, as well as visiting road companies and individual stars. In addition to Bernhardt, E. S. Willard, Robert Loraine, Julia Marlowe and E. H. Sothern appeared on the stage with actors from such companies as *Mrs. Wiggs of the Cabbage Patch, The Three Graces, Before and After, Mexicana,* and *The College Widow.* Members of the Chicago theatrical services—advertisers, stage hands, electricians—all donated their time. The American Federation of Musicians allowed their members to participate in a 500 piece band that played in full uniform outside the tent before the show.

Madame Bernhardt performed in a tent one more time before she left the country. *Camille* was offered on June 9 in Springfield, Mass., because the Syndicate had barred her from its four theatres in that city. This appearance under canvas was said to be the only one in the East. In anticipation of Bernhardt's arrival, promoter George A. Whitney had a tent set up in a field near North End Bridge at a cost of $1,000. However, the tent in which some 2,500 people saw Bernhardt's performance was a far cry from her original "canvas temple." A single setting was used throughout the play, partially obscured by a center pole standing in front of the stage. Outside, trolley cars and automobile horns interfered with the speeches of the actors. And tickets for the performance were sold out of an adjacent coal office.

Sarah Bernhardt's tent that had made history in Dallas and served in Chicago on behalf of the quake victims was shipped to San Francisco for use as a temporary theatre. Along with many other playhouses in San Francisco, the Central Theatre on Eighth and Market Streets had been destroyed by fire. The tent was erected on that site in the heart of the burned out district. Proprietors Howell and Dodge named it the Park Theatre; and on June 6 the doors opened for the first real dramatic performance since the disaster. The bill offered *Hearts of Tennessee*, written by Californian Ulric Collins, for which the stage "was established very artistically and set so pretty with a cottage and a lilac bush that the audience applauded just to see the curtain go up once more on a real play."[19] The tent became once again the "temple" Madame Bernhardt had envisioned. Theatregoers, hungry for entertainment, flocked to the Park, seeming to care little "whether their favorite plays were presented under a roof or under canvas." For months after the Park's opening San Franciscans filled the place night after night. As one reporter observed,

It is a weird sight, after the play is over, to see the throng of play-goers come
pushing through the brilliantly lighted entrance to the tent theatre—out into
the waste of the debris and ashes where there was once the great thoroughfare
of Market Street.[20]

From the time of its spectacular opening in Cycle Park until it
gave way to a permanent structure at Eighth and Market Streets, the
stretch of rope and canvas originally commissioned by Sarah Bernhardt received national recognition as a portable playhouse. It had
served under extraordinary circumstances. And because of widespread publicity attracted by the magic name of Bernhardt, tent
theatres began to lose the taint of the "disreputable" circus and
medicine show; for Bernhardt had played in a tent, and Bernhardt
was the world's greatest living actress.

PLATE 1. Vermontville, Michigan, Opera House, built about 1897. Note fire house at left and council chambers behind telephone pole.

PLATE 2. Traverse City, Michigan, Grand Opera House, with commercial space on street level and offices on upper levels facing the street.

PLATE 3. Lee Avenue Theatre, Brooklyn, a former roller-skating rink altered by repertoire manager, Corse Payton and wife, Etta Reid are encircled above. (copied from New York *Dramatic Mirror*, December 23, 1905, p. xlii.)

PLATE 4. Interior of small town opera house typical of hundreds erected throughout America.

PLATE 5. Same as Plate 4. Note the stock house scenery, a "center door fancy," suitable for numerous plays used by touring repertoire companies.

PLATE 6. Young's Garden Airdome, Terre Haute, Indiana, erected about 1906. Note it was built on what was formerly an empty lot between two store buildings, probably right in the center of the commercial district.

PLATE 7. Interior view of above. (Both copied from *Billboard*, January 30, 1909).

PLATE 8. Board fence which served as sidewall for the typical inexpensive air-dome construction.

PLATE 9. Ricketts' Amphitheatre, Philadelphia, circa 1790. Note shape of construction is similar to the canvas circus round tops of the early 19th century (San Antonio Public Library).

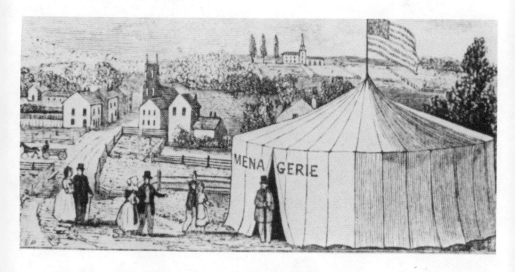

PLATE 10. Early 19th century menagerie tent similar to the circus round top (New York Public Library).

BARNUM'S MAMMOTH TENT.

PLATE 11. P. T. Barnum's Great Asiatic Caravan, Museum and Menagerie tent (1851), 110 feet long (San Antonio Public Library).

PLATE 12. A lithographic artist's concept of Barnum's Great Traveling World's Fair, advertised as having "Two Separate Rival Rings under a vast center-pole pavillion with seats for 14,000." (Library of Congress)

PLATE 13. Early tent theatre, circa 1898, managed by John Ginnivan. Note the use of the word *Opera*.

PLATE 14. Trio Uncle Tom's Cabin Company, an overland tent show. Photograph taken at Lake Webster, Indiana, 1914.

SARAH BERNHARDT IN FRONT OF THE GREAT TENT, CYCLE PARK, DALLAS, TEXAS

Sarah Bernhardt's Triumphant Tour in the We

PLATE 15. Sarah Bernhardt and her famous tent, 1906, Dallas, Texas.

PLATE 16. Improvised stage arrangement of the Bernhardt tent, not completely erected, 1906, Dallas, Texas.

PLATE 17. Park Theatre, San Francisco, at its opening on June 30, 1907. This is the Bernhardt tent placed on the site of the burned down Central Theatre, Eighth and Market Streets, which served as a temporary theatre until a permanent structure could be erected.

PLATE 18. Dramatic tent adapted from the circus round end tent. The poles on either side of the proscenium opening meet above to hold the peak of the canvas, an improvisation designed to do away with the obstructing center pole. (*Billboard*, December 2, 1905).

PLATE 19. Improvised dramatic end still in use in 1927. Longer quarter poles are utilzed at the stage end to raise the canvas to the height necessary for dramatic necessities.

PLATE 20. Interior design for Driver's Improved Theatrical Tent, United States Tent and Awning Company, Chicago, 1910. (*Billboard*, August 27, 1910)

PLATE 21. Same as above. Note the elimination of quarter poles to furnish a clear view of the stage.

PLATE 22. Gemier's Portable Theatre, a French tent show, 1911 (*Current Literature*, LI, October, 1911).

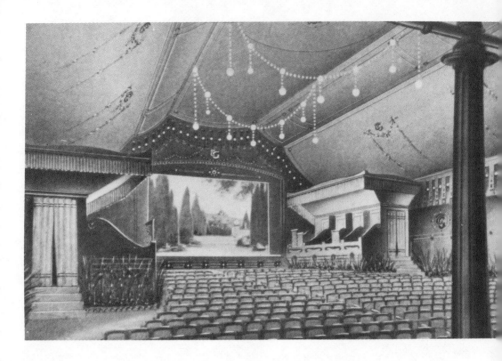

PLATE 23. Sketch of Gemier's Portable Theatre. Note the attempt to simulate the interior of the permanent playhouses (*Theatre*, XI, May, 1911).

PLATE 24. The typical brown Chautauqua tent, with sides open for summer comfort.

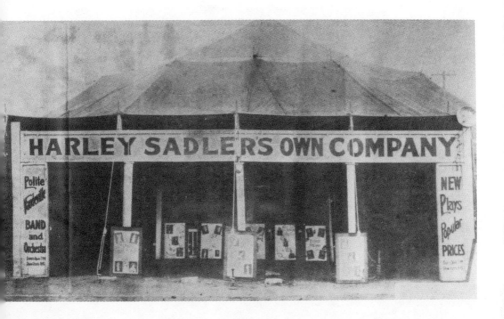

PLATE 25. Theatre lobby display for Harley Sadler's Texas show. This was one of the most successful repertoire tent troupes on the road (*The Sunday Oregonian*, Portland, Oregon, December 21, 1952).

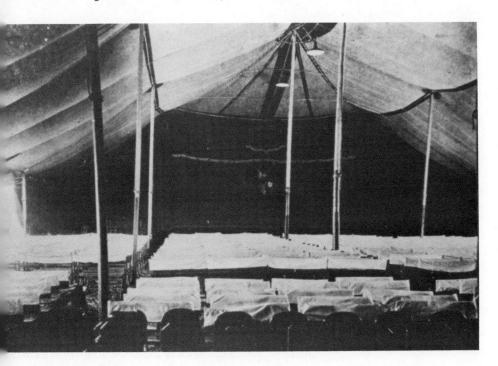

PLATE 26. Aulger Brothers' tent of the 1920's, a standard design of the era of tent show maturity.

PLATE 27. Obrecht Stock Company, a Minnesota troupe comprised mostly of the Obrecht family. (circa 1930)

PLATE 28. Exterior of Frontispiece. Note the extension of the tent's sidewall to allow air circulation (this is called airdoming).

PLATE 29. Thomas Wignell as Jonathan in "The Contrast." Only a partial view is shown of this sketch by William Dunlap for the frontispiece of the play publsihed by subscription in 1790.

PLATE 30. Thomas Wignell as Darby in "Darby's Return," sketched by William Dunlap (1789).

PLATE 31. An 18th century precursor of the Toby character, Mr. Dodd as Abel Drugger in Ben Johnson's *Alchymist*, from a print for the British Library, Strand, 1791.

PLATE 32. The first tent show Toby, Fred Wilson, the most natural in appearance of all Toby comedians.

PLATE 33. The cowboy Toby of Harler Sadler, especially geared for a West Texas audience.

PLATE 34. The early Toby make-up of Neil Schaffner, 1926. Schaffner was one of the best known Tobys of late years.

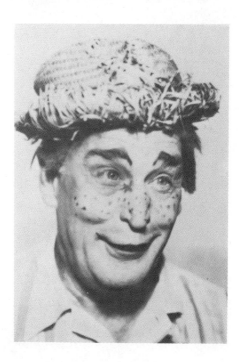

PLATE 35. Schaffner's Toby of the 1950's, illustrating, when compared with PLATE 34, the trend toward a grotesque make-up, changing the country boy into a clown.

PLATE 36. Rose Melville in the role she made famous, Sis Hopkins (New York *Dramatic Mirror*, January 14, 1899).

PLATE 37. The "G-String" character of Guy Hickman.

PLATE 38. In contrast to PLATE 37, L. Verne Slout's "G-String" is dressed in cast-off uniform remnants.

PLATE 39. An early season disaster, a snow down in Vermontville, Michigan, 1927, of the Slout Players' new tent.

PLATE 40. Old print showing the circus bandwagon.

PLATE 41. In contrast, a 1917 dramatic tent show, the Ed C. Nutt Comedy Players, using the circus-style bandwagon at Ft. Smith, Arkansas (*Billboard*, September 1, 1917).

PLATE 42. Band of Murphy's Comedians, a Louisiana troupe, 1911. The cornetist in the front row is Merle Evans, the reknowned band leader for Ringling Brothers' circus.

PLATE 43. The uniformed band of the Rentfrow's Jolly Pathfinders repertoire company.

PLATE 44. The Esler Stock Company, 1894, probably assembled for a street parade.

PLATE 45. The baseball team of the Murphy's Comedians, circa 1914, with manager Horace Murphy.

PLATE 46. Overland travels of the Whitney Wagon Circus, 1880.

PLATE 47. The John Ginnivan Opera Company, a dramatic tent show, moving on farm wagons in 1898.

PLATE 48. Billing like a circus; about a 36-sheet stand of lithograph for this early tent repertoire company.

CHAPTER VI. THE WAR YEARS

FOR THE REPERTOIRE TENT SHOWS, THE MOST SIGNIFICANT DEVELOP-
ments in the second decade of the 20th century were World War I and
the emergence of motor transportation as an American way of life.
Generally speaking, the war years brought prosperity to tent show
managers the like of which they had never experienced. On the other
hand, antagonisms toward show people surfaced in many small communities and resulted in actors being branded as slackers and anti-
patriots. Increasing use of railroad facilities for war needs caused
transportation problems that led to a switch to motor vehicles;
motor truck and trailer became the standard means of moving show
equipment. And, finally, as the war ended, the tent show industry,
assisted by the increasing use of the automobile, had expanded to
the point where it was difficult to find enough actors to meet the
need.

Show business is traditionally a beneficiary of war; the desire to
escape, if only momentarily, from the ugly realities of the day has
always filled wartime theatres. Thus, the World War I years were
the most prosperous in the history of the tents. Although the start
of the European conflict caused a slight recession in America, by
1915 the economy was beginning to accelerate. Industry was getting

into full gear on Allied war orders, and agriculture was finding new markets abroad. Trade with the Allies increased from a 1914 level of $825 million to $3,214 million in 1916. With good crop prices and the prospect of their going even higher, the American farmer was in the mood for amusement. Rural show business boomed. The number of tent shows on the road rose continually as more and more managers entered the field to share in the wartime bonanza. By 1919 *Billboard* was reporting a "tremendous" growth in repertoire, with small companies enlarging their rosters and with many actors going into business for themselves. An editorial declared magnificently that

Our fame has been spread into the remotest corners of the earth. Small repertoire companies carrying the drama and music into towns and villages which had never before witnessed the like. Education, art, morals, ideas, all improved, giving us greater recognition which in turn gives us the right to demand a place far at the top of showdom.[1]

Billboard reported a few months later that the success of the previous summer had "acted with the stimulus of a gold rush." Preparations for the 1920 summer season were so frenzied in February (an early start for most tent managers) that Chicago agent A. Milo Bennett already had orders for plays and people from more than one hundred shows. "According to Mr. Bennett," stated the reporter, "the number of tented attractions will exceed that of any previous season." Bennet went so far as to predict that a "better class" of actors, receiving higher salaries than ever before, would be engaged. He also suggested that many companies would be playing in larger cities with engagements lasting as long as four weeks because of "the scarcity of opera houses, the inroads of pictures in the theatres having reached proportions where other means of presenting productions have become mandatory."[2]

Prosperity did not come without sacrifice. In the first place, the draft took male actors, musicians and canvasmen of prime age. Nationally, over nine and a half million men between the ages of 21 and 31 were registered in 1917; and Congress extended the age limits to 18 and 45 a year later. In all, draft registration included 44 percent of the American male population, with over two and a half million being taken into the armed forces. Tent show musicians and canvasmen were usually young and well within the limits for conscription; for them there was no occupational deferment. Consequently, shows were tapped hard. Drafted canvasmen were of particular concern for tent managers because it meant a smaller and less efficient labor force and created the necessity of hiring local help, usually old men and young boys.

In many communities war fever led to feelings of resentment toward traveling companies. Hostile attitudes were often advanced by local Defense Committees. In 1916 a Committee of National Defense consisting of six cabinet officers and an Advisory Commission of the country's most able businessmen was organized in Washington. Since cabinet members were busy with other problems, the Advisory Commission, entrusted with most of the administration, set up 184,000 local councils in cities, counties and small communities that "transmitted to the people the needs of the government and reflected back to Washington the moods of the people."[3] Frequently these local organizations were over-zealous; their duties, which were vague from the start, were often assumed in excess of authority. "Flying squads" were used to harass farmers into buying war bonds; if demands were refused, farm houses were splashed with yellow paint. "He who is not with us is against us!" seems to have been the attitude, with reason cast asunder. In Pocatello, Idaho, a railroad clerk who had ventured the opinion that the Germans would win the war was taken from his office and handcuffed to a telegraph pole in the main part of town. His exhibition attracted a crowd from which came shouts of "Why don't you hang him!" Actor Luke Cosgrave, a witness to the disgusting scene, observed, "These proceedings made us understand that we really were at war and idle words might be answered by mob violence at any time."[4] Tent show manager A. F. Fanshawe informed the *Billboard* in 1918 that Defense Councils in Oklahoma and Texas had caused the closing of "several of the repertoire companies which had been known on the highway for many years." In referring to flagrant abuse of power by local committees, Bert Chipman, who toured with the Sells-Floto Circus at this time, noted, "They treated the city laws and ordinances as a joke and ran everything to suit themselves." Judging that they did more harm than good, Chipman found some committee members were opposed to all forms of amusement except church functions and Chautauquas. On the other hand, he conceded, there were committeemen who were "public spirited" and who "handled everything in a true businesslike manner."[5]

Navasota, Texas, was the scene of a particularly inhospitable act. After Rentfrow's Jolly Pathfinders had finished setting up their show tent, the manager was visited by members of the local committee who warned him not to give a performance in their town. J. N. Rentfrow explained that he had paid his war tax and state tax and county and city licenses and tried to convince them that to lay off for a week would be a financial hardship for him. The committee replied that there had been a money drain on the town from the sale of War Saving Stamps and that the townspeople did not desire a further depletion. To make certain there would be no performance that evening, the committee stationed sentries at streets leading to the show lot. With such odds against him, Rentfrow could do nothing but close. However, on the second day, the local men returned and "virtually arrested every male member of the company" and required them to show proof of draft registration.

Still another difficulty was the scarcity of good show lots. An important consideration for any company was the tent's location, preferably as close to the center of town as possible, and in the direction traffic customarily flowed. But because of war demands, all available space was devoted to "war gardens," sometimes making it necessary to leave out a canvas middle piece to squeeze onto a small lot.

Before the war, most established tent shows traveled by rail, utilizing coach, pullman, and baggage car in the manner of the opera house companies, carrying actors, wardrobe trunks, and scenery on a single contract. Here again, the circus was the forerunner that set transportation policies. A circus owned by Charles Bacon and Edwin Derious appears to have been the earliest amusement to move by rail in America; this occurred in 1838, only ten years after the first railroad was established in this country. However, it was impractical at this time to commit a show to extensive rail travel because the variation in rail gauge from one line to the next made it impossible to use cars that had wheels fitted to a single gauge size. Where rails were incompatible it was necessary to laboriously transfer equipment from one car to another. Before rail travel could be completely feasible there had to be access to all parts of the country. Prior to the Civil War, railroad networks adequately served the eastern half of the country; then, following the war, the roads began stretching westward and in many cases moved ahead of the expanding frontier. In

1865 the Great Plains and Rocky Mountain regions had only 960 miles of line; in the next fifty years, some 90,000 miles. By 1880 the national mileage totalled 93,000. Energetic expansion, ultimately sparked by World War I necessities, raised that figure to an all-time mark of 254,000 miles of railroad line from coast to coast in 1916. Nonetheless, records show some railroad circuses in operation before the Civil War: the Railroad Circus and Crystal Amphitheatre exhibited in Detroit in 1853; Den Stone's Original Railroad Circus was there the following year; and in 1856, Spalding and Rogers were out under the title of Railroad Circus. Yet, all experiments with rail travel were short lived until after the war and until, in 1868, Dan Costello's Circus and Menagerie made the first transcontinental tour. But as competition between the large circuses forced them to become veritable cities under canvas, with wagon after wagon of equipment and livestock, rail travel became necessary. It was a complicated procedure, demanding pre-season planning of itineraries, arranging time schedules and co-ordinating rail routing between lines.

Rail transportation was made even more attractive for touring companies when the railroads offered theatrical rate concessions. The average house repertoire troupe, for example, could transport an entire outfit for the price of the coach fares. With the purchase of twenty-five tickets at a reduced rate of two cents a mile, a baggage car was supplied without cost. If a second car was required, it could be obtained for an additional fifteen cents a mile. But for most shows, a single car was all that was needed for trunks and scenic equipment. Ted North used a single 70-foot baggage car for transporting his show property.[6] In contrast, the Jennings Dramatic Company, touring Texas in 1917, moved on two coaches, two pullmans, and a combination baggage car.[7] Actors usually rode in the public coaches. The more prosperous managers owned a private car in which they lived with their family. Each of the Seven Cairns Brothers, for many years proprietors of a one-night stand tent show, owned a private pullman that was considered a "veritable palace on wheels."[8]

Railroads encountered car and locomotive shortages by 1917 because of the urgent demands of war. Large numbers of troops, as well as tons of raw materials, agricultural products, and vast amounts of equipment, had to be moved. America was responsible for both its own needs and for an increasing commitment to its European Allies. The bulk of shipments travelled from the West to the East to be loaded onto boats for overseas destinations. In the fall, there were some 180,000 loaded railway cars backed up on the eastern ports awaiting designation. When the railroads attempted to remedy the shortage by purchasing new cars, delays were caused by manufacturers' involvement in other war equipment. To increase railroad efficiency, all services not necessary for national defense were curtailed: trains were consolidated, schedules were tightened, freight service was suspended unless good cause could be shown.

The pressure placed on railroads to accommodate the increasing demands of war was reflected in the mounting transportation problems of tent shows. For example, Angell's Comedians were forced to cancel a planned winter tour of the South when the Illinois Central Railroad refused to move them; the baggage car lease owned by the railroad was suspended because of increasing war necessities. In 1919 the Florence Players closed an excellent tour due to "unsatisfactory railroad connections." Manager Hicker was quoted as saying that "never before in all his vast experience in show business has he had so much difficulty in arranging railroad jumps."[9] Companies that owned their own railroad cars found them frequently sidetracked to make way for strategic materials. Inconsistencies in time schedules and rising passenger and freight rates forced many troupes to hire rigs in each town to move the show overland. Because tent show managers could no longer depend on the railroads, they turned to motor vehicles as a solution to their transportation woes.

Trucks were placed on the market for wide commercial use around 1911. In that year Avery trucks were advertised for both city and count hauling, with optional hard rubber tires or cast steel rim wheels. And General Motors announced a line of trucks with either gasoline or electric powered engines: the Model H, with 3½ ton capacity, was priced (chassis only) at $3,500; the Model S, 2 ton capacity, sold (chassis only) for $2,750. The Lincoln Motor Car Works offered light delivery cars, "furnished with either open or panel-top bodies," for prices from $575 to $785.[10] The switch to motor transportation was an expensive one for the repertoire companies to make. Certainly, the decision by each manager came from a pressing necessity to find some means other than difficult railroads.

One of the first repertoire managers to foresee war transportation problems was Frank Ginnivan who opened his 1915 season with six trucks and five touring cars. But, again, the circus led the way in pioneering motor vehicles. In 1905, Howard Starrett used an advanced car and four modified automobile buggies. By 1917, "Lucky Bill" Newton's show was equipped with cars for transporting the personnel and for pulling sleeping trailers. And, finally, with the large United States Motorized Circus, which was organized for the summer of 1918, the "automobile circus" became a reality. Motor vehicles, some as wide as seven feet, pulled trailers nearly as large. They formed a caravan that functioned much the same as a circus train; traveling in three sections, with a fleet totaling 175 cars, trucks and trailers, the United States Motorized Circus was the equivalent of a 100-car railroad show. Moving at a speed of twelve miles per hour, the circus averaged twenty-five to thirty mile jumps. The performers lived in sleeping trailers similar to the railroad pullman car. To keep the autos rolling, each caravan section was supplied with gasoline tank trucks and repair wagons; and a "pathfinder car" went on ahead to locate the best roads and firmest bridges.[11] By 1918, such standard troupes as the Norma Ginnivan Stock Company, George Sweet Players, Amazon Brothers, Shannon Stock Company, Hugo Players, Princess Stock Company, Ripple and Lee Repertoire Company, and William F. Lewis Stock Company had purchased trucks, trailers and touring cars and were expressing satisfaction in circumventing the rise of railroad rates and the uncertainties of railroad schedules. The changeover continued until, eventually, all repertoire outfits were moved by this method.

The Lanshaw Players performing in small towns "somewhere in Michigan" in the summer of 1918 reported that business was extremely good: "Where they all come from, no one can tell. All one can say is, thanks to Henry Ford."[12] Tent shows were beginning to benefit from the growing public use of the automobile. In 1906 it was considered a plaything of the wealthy; but within a few years the middle class began to take interest. The automobile emerged as a useful machine, not just a novelty, until by 1920 there were over nine million car registrations in the country. As it became more reliable and less expensive to own and operate, as road mileage increased, and as more garages and gas stations appeared along the highways, the automobile wedged itself into the farmer's way of life. Such slogans as "I'd rather do without clothes than without a car!" and "You can't drive to town in a bathtub!" became common defenses of car ownership.

The automobile enabled the farmer to enlarge his social and recreational activities. He could crank up his Model T after doing the chores and drive into town in time to attend an evening function, following which he could return home and arrive there at a reasonable hour.

Although the number of shows being formed for the 1921 summer tent season surpassed that of any previous year, show business was in for a slump. The wartime economy could not be maintained; falling farm prices proved incompatible with soaring land values which were up seventy percent by 1919. When government support of wheat was withdrawn in 1920, wheat prices sank from a wartime level of $2.00 a bushel to 67 cents by the end of the year. Farmers who had borrowed money to expand their holdings could not pay the interest on their loans. Bankruptcies and foreclosures increased sharply. A total of 433,000 farmers lost their farms as the boom "turned into the worst agricultural depression the nation had ever known."[13] The *Billboard* reported as late as mid-July that managers were still hanging around the repertoire centers of Chicago with their "ears to the ground," waiting day by day to decide whether or not to form their companies. Never in the history of the repertoire business had shows been so late in organizing. After a period of wartime prosperity that had enabled many shows to refurbish and replace old equipment, to pay off previous debts, and to operate, perhaps for the first time, in a financially secure manner, after a prosperity that accounted for large numbers of new managers entering the field, the tent shows in the summer of 1921 were faced with a recession that marked the end of the golden years of growth and development.[14]

CHAPTER VII. TENT SHOW DRAMAS

THE GREATER PART OF THE DRAMATIC LITERATURE USED UNDER
canvas during the years being considered consisted of plays carried
over from opera house repertoire and of new or revised pieces re-
flecting contemporary notions. Although investigation is difficult
because of the managerial practice of freely changing titles, it can
be determined that the body of plays used under canvas were: 1)
aged melodramas unprotected by copyright, 2) pirated New York
successes, 3) and comedy-dramas written by tent show people. Many
of the old stand-bys were such perennials as *Kathleen Mavourneen,
Camille, East Lynne, Caprice, Fanchon the Cricket, The Hidden
Hand*, and *Jack Sheppard*. Another popular practice was the dramatization of contemporary novels to take advantage of a public obsession for "best sellers"; favorites included Charlotte M. Braeme's sensational love romance, *Dora Thorne*, along with her *Thorns and
Orange Blossoms*, Mary J. Holmes' *Lena Rivers*, Kate Douglas Wiggin's
Rebecca of Sunnybrook Farm, George Barr McCutcheon's *Graustark*,
John Fox's *Trail of the Lonesome Pine*, and Wright's *Shepherd of the
Hills*. Local color themes appealed to small town audiences, particularly "rube dramas" tailored to rural tastes, portraying Victorian
ideals of virtue, reverence for mother, home, and heaven, suspicion

of everything urban, and changing social and cultural attitudes within the tight control of 19th century morality. Characters conformed to the image the rural dweller had created of himself. Exterior settings were popular, but farm kitchens, cabins in the north woods and western range supplied familiar atmospheres as well. With such emphasis on local color, characters tended to become stock; the local pastor, the fallen woman, the gossip, the silly kid and the shrewd town eccentric found their way into play after play. Eventually, the silly kid and his female counterpart became identified as Toby and Sis Hopkins; and the old eccentric assumed the slang name of G-String because of the customary chin whiskers used by the character actors portraying the roles.

Sis Hopkins was taken from the famous character portrayal by Rose Melville, who performed in the role for many years. After gaining acting experience in the Baldwin-Melville Stock Company, playing a variety of characters ranging from Topsy to Louise in *The Two Orphans*, Rose appeared in 1894 with her sister, Ida, in a specialty act at the Garden Theatre, New York City, called "Two Little Jays from Indiana." Her next engagement was as Dolly Bond in *The Prodigal Father*, a role she performed for two years. A specialty act in the last part of the play featuring Sis Hopkins was an impressive contrast to Dolly. In 1898, Miss Melville joined the touring *By the Sad Sea Waves*, a "rag-time opera" produced by Mathews and Bulgar, and "without her name even appearing on the program, she received the praise of the press and was an instant hit."[1]

She went on without a rehearsal and the eccentric make-up and strange lines gave the members of the company such a surprise that they could not restrain their mirth, and laughed just as loudly as anyone in the audience.[2]

The management immediately expanded her part into a principal role, which resulted in instant success and the creation of a new star.

Everywhere the company has been, the newspapers have waxed enthusiastic over Miss Melville's work, and her engagements have been a series of triumphs, winding up in her great New York success.[3]

After *By the Sad Sea Waves* finished the New York run, Rose Melville continued her portrayal of Sis Hopkins for several years. There was a tour of vaudeville with *Sis Hopkins' Visit*, written by Carroll Fleming. Later, Fleming wrote a full length play for her, *Sis Hopkins, A Wise Child*. Finally, the character was written into an old play authored by Rose's brother-in-law, Samuel Young, *Zeb, the Clodhopper* (sometimes called *Zeb*). The fame from her continual portrayals linked her inseparably to the role and set a style that was imitated by soubrettes for many years.[4] The little jay from Indiana, with pigtailed hair, shapeless dress, and hanging petticoat, became so identified with the character that comedy country girl roles in tent show plays were often called Sis Hopkins parts.

The origins of the G-String character are more obscure. As can best be determined, it is a development of a variety of eccentric old rural philosophers that followed after the success of Josh Whitcomb— Si Plunkard, Si Stebbins, and Josh Simpkins. The G-String was shrewd, honest, brash, and inventive. He wore the chin whiskers of the stereotyped rube. Sometimes he was dressed in remnants of Civil War uniform. Sometimes he represented the office of village constable, or worked as drayman or depot attendant, handyman or janitor, wearing ill-fitting garb identifiable with the particular pastime. Like the silly kid, his responsibility was to provoke laughter through his rural eccentricities. His roots were in 19th century drama. The Yankee character, which has received a fair share of attention by historians, was the precursor of modern local color low comedy. Dorson has suggested that the 19th century Yankee led to the vein of homely, philosophical, older men, epitomized by Josh Whitcomb, or, in his words, "the sentimental sage."

The Yankee slipped insensibly into a new role; the brash bumpkin aged into a country philosopher. . . . The quondam champion of outnumbered armies and outraged heroines now played a quieter part unraveling domestic triangles and setting a good example. In the sense that his blatant heroics have been softened to a heroism of a more spiritual and plausible sort, the character reflected the gathering culture, the urban temperament, and the Victorian standards of audiences in the '80's and '90's. The American theatre, and Jonathan with it, showed by 1900 signs of maturity.[5]

Sis Hopkins and the G-String did not attain the popularity of the silly kid. They remained amusing and favorable small town images, "second bananas," restricted perhaps by sex and age and limited by the playwright's pen. Generally, although they repeatedly appeared in tent show dramas, they did not acquire a continuing identity from one play to the next. In contrast, the silly kid became so enthusiastically accepted by small town audiences that his given name, Toby, was used by comedians on the street as well as on the stage.

The success of Denman Thompson's *The Old Homestead* was responsible for a flood of rural dramas. Thompson's play was first produced at the Boston Museum on April 5, 1886. A New York engagement followed at the Fourteenth Street Theatre beginning January 10, 1887. With the author in the leading role of Josh Whitcomb, the play continued to be popular throughout the country until Thompson's death in 1911. Success is said to have been almost solely due to the lovable Josh, who was developed by Thompson for a sketch first performed in 1876. According to Quinn, the character was based on a real person, Joshua Holbrook of Swansea, New Hampshire.[6] The natural acting of Thompson, a former variety hall performer, and the eccentric, homely demeanor of Josh Whitcomb created a model stage image for imitators who during the next three decades amused American audiences with a variety of rube philosophers. Rural melodramas with homespun comedy followed under such titles as *Sis Hopkins*, *Old Dan Tucker*, *Old Si Stebbins*, *Ole Olsen*, *Si Plunkard*, *Uncle Hez*, *Uncle Josh Spruceby*, *Yon Yonson*, *The Village Postmaster*, and *The Village Parson*. Exploitation of rural drama was apparent as late as 1905 when a writer to the *Billboard* commented that New York State was being overrun with "rube shows"—*Quincy Adams Sawyer*, *The Missouri Girl*, *Eben Holden*, *Old Si Stebbins*, *Joshua Simpkins*, *Way Down East*, and *Mugg's Landing*. Unquestionably, patrons of small town opera houses were receptive to dramatizations of small town life at the very time when tent shows were being organized in numbers. It only follows that repertoire managers continued to satisfy this public whim when they moved under canvas.

Throughout the years, audiences grew tired of the old melodramas; and revised copyright laws became more punitive toward managers and actors performing plays without authorization. Therefore, tent show people began writing plays for themselves, using shorter casts and fewer set requirements; and, at the same time, making them more relevant to small town life. Charles Harrison was one of the most successful tent show playwrights; he knew what appealed to rural audiences. His most popular piece, *Saintly Hypocrites and Honest Sinners*, was performed by every show on the road from 1915 to the present. The play's effectiveness is made evident by the following commendation from Charles T. Mills, editor of the Montevideo (Minnesota) *American*.

This is a very appropriate offering for any community and especially so for Montevideo. . . . It portrays a living picture of society as it is carried on today by a certain class with a more "holy than thou" spirit strongly in the foreground. Nothing coarse or vulgar, just an amusing and enjoyable entertainment with a forcible living lesson of everyday life. All church members should see it, especially those sincere in their faith and seeking an honest spiritual social growth in the community. The preachers of town should unite and arrange with the community to give the play Sunday evening in place of their regular sermons. At least they should all see it this afternoon at the Eagle Theatre.[7]

Another example of the play's success occurred in Topeka, Kansas, where the North Brothers Stock Company was performing in tent stock. Topeka audiences were accustomed to high-class New York bills; but when *Saintly Hypocrites* was presented "it was written up as the acme of the season." From that time on, the North company used Harrison plays and "always did good business."[8]

Saintly Hypocrites was ideal for tent shows. The play could be easily mounted and transported. The single setting was placed in the parlor of a small town parsonage. The costumes were contemporary. The ten-people cast—six men and four women—included recognizable characters such as a village gossip, over-pious deacons with questionable business dealings, the scorned daughter of the town drunkard, a good-natured handyman, a well intentioned and respected minister, and maverick youngsters. The plot was simple and melodramatic. Rev. Richard Dean and his wife, Fanny, are comfortably settled in a community that has erected a new church. The church is controlled by its board chairman and mortgage holder, Deacon Stromberg. Fletcher, formerly a prosperous farmer, has fallen into drunken ways and, as a result, has lost his farm to Stromberg. When Rev. Dean is informed that Fletcher, on his death bed, has requested to see him, Dean, giving in to pressure from Stromberg and his cronies, Deacon Malcolm and Sister Higgens, ignores Fletcher's summons. The worldly brother of the minister, Billie, just returned after a ten year absence, proves that Christian deeds are practiced outside the church as well as within by going to the bedside of Fletcher in place of the Rev. Dean. Fletcher confides to Billie that Stromberg started him on the downward path of drink and tried to seduce his daughter, Mary. The battle Rev. Dean wages between his conscience and his desire for material comfort is finally won to the satisfaction of small town audiences. He defies Stromberg, Malcolm and Higgens by offering to preside over Fletcher's funeral. And, in a dramatic final scene, Billie reveals the dying Fletcher's accusations. The church hypocrites are defeated and Rev. and Mrs.

Dean retain the respect of the community.[9]

Harrison wrote a second "preacher bill' a few years after *Saintly Hypocrites* titled *The Only Road*, which included similar characters and much the same statement concerning hypocrisy. The Rev. Frank Curtis just engaged by the church board is a man with liberal views and a strong sense of right. He opposes the questionable practices of some members of the congregation and stands firm against pressure from such prominent people as the local banker, a well-to-do merchant, and the church gossip. When Curtis proposes that a club house be built where young people can dance and put on entertainments, the over-pious church members set up resistance; Curtis is accused of putting ideas of "new fangled nonsense" in the minds of the town's youth. At a meeting called to prefer charges against him, Rev. Curtis lectures the trouble-making board members about the un-Christian conduct of their own lives, finishing with:

I want all of you to go home; think over what has happened here tonight. Look back into the past and see what Hypocrisy has done for you all. Then look out into the Future and try to realize what happiness and contentment could be yours. Come to Church next Sunday with your minds made up to make a new start. We'll all join hands and prepare ourselves to find the Only Road that leads through Damnation to Eternal Rest and Happiness.[10]

Another Harrison play, *The Awakening of John Slater*, can be ranked with *Saintly Hypocrites* as a tent show classic. *Slater* is a vehicle for one of the most hilarious silly kid roles, Lun Slater, in all of tent show literature. Every Toby comedian has played Lun more times than he can recall. Copyrighted in 1914, the play was written a few years after the stock character of Toby was introduced by Fred Wilson.[11] The story deals with the opposing attitudes of country and city life, dramatically illustrated when Ma and Pa Slater, along with Lun and sister Nan, visit John, who has become a success-ful lawyer in New York City. The inhospitable treatment they receive from John's wife, Adele, supplies substance for a good deal of comedy as Lun responds with brash insults. After Adele is exposed as a profes-sional bigamist, John realizes he is still in love with the girl back home. He declares to his family that "we're all going home tomorrow. I'm going to ask Flora, the girl I love, to marry me. And then we're all coming back here; and this is going to be your home."[12]

George J. Crawley was another early writer of tent show bills. If *The Girl of the Flying X* were his only contribution, he would still deserve mention; for this play, better known as *Sputters*, contains a silly kid role rivalled only by *Lun Slater* for popularity among Toby comics. Sputters is a stuttering cowboy. The story, set outside Colonel Bailey's ranch house, deals with a mysterious ranch foreman, a Mexican cattle rustler, and Colonel Bailey's daughter, Rose, who is in love with the foreman. But all this takes a back seat to the antics of Sputters. Rose teaches Sputters to overcome his stuttering by drawing an imaginary square with his finger, each side of the square to be drawn in time with each syllable he utters. By repeating the movements, making the square over and over, he can talk for extended periods without stuttering. For an imaginative comedian, this device unleashes endless possibilities. Along with *Saintly Hypocrites* and *John Slater*, *Sputters* remained a part of tent show repertoire for as long as there were shows to perform it.

Hundreds of plays were written by writers employed by the Chicago Manuscript Company. The company, owned by Alex Byers, is referred to in an earlier chapter dealing with play piracy. In 1909 Congress passed the Currier Bill which contained all of the best of the previous copyright laws, plus stipulations enabling the punishment of the "dealers" in unauthorized manuscripts. Provisions were included for "prompt apprehension and punishment of play pirates and of persons who maintain places in which typewritten manuscripts are sold without authority." The punishment was made a misdemeanor and called for imprisonment of not more than one year and a fine of not less than one hundred dollars or more than one thousand dollars, or both.[13] These restrictions led to a change in Byers' business practice; for beginning in 1909 the Chicago Manuscript Company served tent managers as a "legitimate" play brokerage. Byers' stable of writers included Myron Leffingwell, W. C. Herman, Nelson Compston, Clarence Black, and Langdale Williams. There were many others, some who made copies of recent shows and revamped them into pieces that could be sold to tent show managers under other titles. A few of his hack writers were drunks who, for one hundred dollars or so, wrote plays, most of which were registered for copyright under Byers' name.

Herman authored and doctored many pieces; but the two most popular with tent show managers were *Clouds and Sunshine* and *Call of the Woods*. The first will be discussed in the next chapter because of its significance in popularizing the Toby character. *Call of the Woods*, which was still being staged under canvas in the 1950's, is

replete with melodramatic speeches and simple moralizing. The single
setting represents the interior of a cabin in the Canadian north woods.
Blind Mrs. Hughes is the mother of two half-brothers. She prefers
Willis, who has studied for the ministry, over Dave, a simple, unpol-
ished soul. "There is no doubt about Willis," she exclaims, "for he's
a model young man. Honest, upright, and God fearing. But Dave—
the less we say of him, the better."[14] Money has been stolen in the
household. Mrs. Hughes erroneously suspects Dave; however, Willis
has really been lifting the cash to cover pressing gambling debts. The
rivalry between the two brothers is complicated by the love each feels
for Doris Keene, who has recently returned to Moose Jaw after a time
away at school. To smear his brother, Willis convinces Doris that Dave
is romantically involved with a half-breed Indian girl employed in the
Hughes home. At the dramatic finish of the first act, Dave is turned
out by his irate mother. However, his parting shot assures us of his
true nature.

You may drive me from you if you wish, mother, but I'll keep on loving you
because you *are* my mother; and if you ever have need for your no-account son,
he'll come back to you if he has to crawl.[15]

Willis has been using the Indian girl to help him in his deceptions.
When she refuses to be a party to further dishonesties, he attempts
to silence her with an axe handle. The blow succeeds in bringing her
to the realization that Willis is not in love with her as he so often con-
fessed, and that he has no intention of taking her away with him.
Ultimately, she clears Dave and involves Willis. And in a final touch-
ing scene, Mrs. Hughes crosses to Dave as she says, "Dave, you are
innocent. My heart and hand are calling you." Doris agrees, "And
so are mine." And as he takes both women in his arms, Dave happily
replies, "And they are better than the call of the woods."[16]

    In assessing the theatrical preferences of small town audiences,
it is useful to turn to the Chautauqua platform; for plays performed
in Chautauqua, which was so successful in rural areas during the years
under discussion, were used by tent show companies as well. Chautauqua programs reflected the themes of "mother, home, and heaven."
This was suggested in speech and song, in the philosophy of Chautauqua's idol—William Jennings Bryan, in the platitudes of its inspirational
lecturers, in the sentiment of its drama. Once introduced to Chautauqua
audiences, plays became so popular, stated Charles Horner, one of the

pioneer managers of tented Chautauqua, that "when we had begun to offer them there was no way to stop."[17] They not only appealed to the regular Chautauqua-goers, but to a new audience; farmers and townspeople not interested in lectures and musical concerts were lured into the brown tents to enjoy what Joseph E. Gould called, "innocuous bits of sunshine."[18]

The Winchell Smith and John E. Hazzard comedy-drama, *Turn to the Right,* was one of the most popular pieces used in Chautauqua, as well as in tent repertoire. It is sentimental, homespun, simple, humorous in terms of low comedy, and clean; it conforms to the ideals of mother, home, and heaven. Joe Bascom had left his mother, his home and his childhood sweetheart to seek a fortune. Desire for wealth led to gambling, drink and the inevitable need to obtain money for both. He turned to robbery for which he was convicted and sent to prison; or so we are led to believe at the outset of the play. As it happens, however, he was "sent up" unjustly. Joe returns home with two ex-convicts, Muggs and Gilly, unfortunates who are potential converts to the good life. On Joe's return, Deacon Tillinger, a wealthy merchant and father of Joe's childhood girl friend, Elsie, is about to foreclose on Mrs. Bascom's farm. Again, the unsympathetic or antagonistic character represents wealth and local church authority. But Tillinger does not remain a villain. He is made to regret his greedy dealings and hypocritical manner as he is tricked at every turn by Joe's penitentiary cronies. Almost over night, he becomes an accepted member of the Bascom family. The fortune Joe sought turns up in his own back yard. Mrs. Bascom's fancy for making preserves from peaches growing on her property is turned to profit. The idea for manufacturing and wholesaling the canned fruit is offered by a country bumpkin type who works in Tillinger's market. Sam is an enterprising youngster, wise-cracking, eccentrically rustic, appearing only sparingly within the story. But when tent shows performed the play, Sam became the stock character, Toby.

The plot is simple, easy to follow, leaving nothing to the imagination. Rural audiences preferred it this way. Characters reflect popular attitudes toward right and wrong, with wrong being disposed of in conformance with Christian practice. The homespun rural dwellers are idealized. Rustic comedy abounds. Filial devotion is stressed. Success through enterprise is encouraged. Deviates from right are allowed back into the fold. Everything is agreeable to the image the auditor has formed of himself and his neighbors, supporting his ideals of mother, home, and heaven.

An important element in tent show drama is what Hofstadter termed the "agrarian myth," representing the "kind of homage that Americans have paid to the fancied innocence of their origins."[19] In the myth, the hero is the yeoman farmer, the ideal man and the ideal citizen; living close to and receiving the benefits of nature; maintaining an integrity and wholesomeness through isolation. The ideal man is simple, honest, independent, enterprising, healthy and happy. This is not to say that rural dwellers conformed to this image; the myth was created outside the community. It was, as Hofstadter explains, a literary idea innovated by an upper-class society of the 18th century who turned to the classic writers for their pastoral ideal. This myth of the sanctity of the soil was perpetuated in early America by such prominent men as Alexander Hamilton, who gave agriculture "pre-eminence over every other kind of industry," and Benjamin Franklin, who termed it "the only honest way" to acquire wealth, "wherein man receives a real increase of the seed thrown into the ground, a kind of continuous miracle, wrought by the hand of God in his favor, as a reward for his innocent life and virtuous industry."[20]

The myth became more emphatic as the farmers' fears multiplied. The great sweep of power, political and financial, from rural to urban areas that occurred in the 19th century as manufacturing began to dominate farming, markedly changed farm life. Self-sufficiency disappeared; the farmer became a businessman, concerned with marketing, transportation, real estate, and a myriad of other complicated dealings. He saw his sons and daughters leaving the quiet, laborious life in the country for a more exciting existence in the city where greater opportunities beckoned. Faced with frightening change, the farmer looked back to what seemed to him the simple, happy days of agriculture, accepting the literary myth and envisioning himself a part of it.

Oddly enough the agrarian myth came to be believed more widely and tenaciously as it became more fictional. At first it was propagated with a kind of genial candor and only later did it acquire overtones of insincerity.[21]

Tent show dramas supported this idealistic image of the farmer. The gossips, the hypocrites, and the dishonest deacons were small town upper-class, not tillers of the soil. The yeoman was their prey, vulnerable through innocence. For him, righteousness was his defense and his strength. The simple way was the honest way. Education connoted insincerity and even dishonesty, as in the case of the half-brother, Willis, in *Call of the Woods*; along with wealth, education was associated with city life.

Hand in hand with the agrarian myth is a country-city antithesis. Not original with tent show drama, the conflict has been a useful plot device in all popular theatre. Shakespeare applied it to delightfully comic success. The Restoration playwrights carried on the practice, exemplified in Wycherley's *The Country Wife*, so brilliantly detailed by Norman Holland.[22] The rube and the city dweller were contrasting images throughout the 19th century in cartoons, monologues, lectures, political speeches, editorials, and magazine stories. The modish attire of the city "feller" with top hat and cane, and perhaps a dainty mustache, formed a familiar stereotype; another was the farmer in straw hat, boots, and chin whiskers, popular among magazine illustrators and vaudeville caricaturists.

In 1890 the population of the United States was 62 million; in ten years the figure had increased to 75 million, with the urban centers feeling the greater growth. At this same time, agrarian population was on the decline. In 1880 about one-fifth of the nation lived in communities of 8,000 or more; by 1900 the ratio had increased to one-third. Urban growth was in part due to accelerated immigration and in part to the influx of farm youth, disenchanted with farm life and enticed by the wages of industry and the pulse of city living. The farmer resented the loss of his children to this new way of life. He was suspicious of foreigners who had arrived in great numbers. He formed a picture of the city as "a home of loan sharks, dandies, fops, and aristocrats with European ideas who despised farmers as hayseeds."[23]

Much of tent show drama reflects rural attitudes toward the city. *John Slater* is just one example of a country boy who left the farm only to be threatened by metropolitan corruption. Single women, who had lived in the city, were frequent targets of suspicion. In *The Only Road*, Rev. Curtis befriends Corrine Blair, a young lady who after the death of her father was forced to work in the city. When she returns to the small town several years later, the money she acquired while away brands her as sinful. Another type of plot brings the city man to the country where he is overcome by the simplicity of its people and the beauty and wholesomeness of its maidens.

The rapid pace of social and cultural change, apparent at the beginning of the 20th century, was reflected in drama. The new century brought with it expressions of newness—the "new theology," the "new morality," the "new woman," the "new immigration," the "new city," and the "new South." Technological advances were responsible for a good deal of change in living habits. The phonograph, the telegraph, the radio, the automobile, and the moving picture penetrated rural life. The modern attitudes of youth, marking a generation gap, are characterized by jazz age slang that befuddles misunderstanding elders. For example, both *Saintly Hypocrites* and *The Only Road* include juvenile and ingenue roles representative of the new freedom of thought and action. The youngsters say what they feel, and they say it in modern idiom. They violate the old notion that children should be seen and not heard; they no longer act in respectful agreement with their elders.

The new freedom was expressed by an obsession with "sex." The phonograph blared such tunes as "Hot Lips," "I Need Lovin'," and "Burning Kisses." "Between the magazines and the movies," one newspaperman observed, "a lot of these little towns seem literally saturated with sex."[24] Tent show dramas reflected this change with such titles as *Why Girls Walk Home, What Every Daughter Should Learn, Up in Mabel's Room,* and *Twin Beds*. Although some of the plays were Broadway successes, others were the same tired Victorian "clap-trap," re-named and renovated in an attempt to keep up-to-date. One observer commented that this sort of thing "ventures to hint of sophistication, to suggest a liberal moral code— but in its offerings virtue invariably triumphs and wicked little girls who go to roadhouses always get punished."[25] The sex play, if one can call it that, with title suggesting bedroom farce, was preferred by tent managers as a closing night attraction. This allowed them to promote it throughout the week and gave the audience a year to get over the disappointment of finding nothing in the play to equal the shocking title.

CHAPTER VIII. THE DEVELOPMENT OF "TOBY" AS
A STOCK CHARACTER

AN IMPORTANT DEVELOPMENT IN TENT REPERTOIRE IS THE GRADUAL take-over by a beloved stock character, Toby, who emerged from the traditional line of theatrical rustics to become a nightly fixture and feature attraction with many companies. The facts concerning his sudden materialization are confusing. It is generally accepted that he grew out of Cal Herman's play, *Clouds and Sunshine*, which contains the comedy role of Tobe Haxton. It appears, however, that *Clouds and Sunshine* is merely a copy of an earlier piece, *Out of the Fold* by Langdon McCormick; and that it was Toby Tompkins, a relatively minor character in McCormick's play who inspired comedian Fred Wilson to call all of his "silly kid" roles "Toby."

Toby, when he emerged as a stock figure, was a redheaded, freckle-faced, country boy, dressed in rural attire—a Huck Finn or Peck's Bad Boy, at various times brash, shy, shrewd, natively bright, stupid, industrious, lazy. He loved a prank, hated sin, supported the ideals of mother, home, and heaven. He was talkative, frequently boastful, using the unpretentious dialect of the region in which he lived. Occasionally, he even stuttered. As *deus ex machina* in many of the tent show bills, Toby was on hand to determine the outcome. As a stock character, he was subject to the style and comic eccentricities of the individual actors who portrayed him. He took on manners of the regions in which he appeared; with some companies he was a mid-western farm boy, with others he was a western cow-hand, or lackadaisical hill-billy. And as the star of many companies, he was molded by business necessity: if an enthusiastic public demanded to see him nightly, Toby was included in all of the bills; if the audience preferred broad comedy, Toby's antics grew more ludicrous and his physical appearance more grotesque. This was particularly the case when performed by comedians who were company managers as well; their Tobys were often overworked and overdone in an attempt to cater to the whims of their audience; to this extent, performances suffered from too-much-Toby. This is apparent when one looks at the style of Toby comedians of recent years; the fresh country boy has succumbed to a more exaggeratedly made-up, a more grotesquely costumed, zany-acting clown who takes over the entire program, pushing the play and the performers into the background.

Toby was many things to the many audiences who adopted him as their own; but basic to all was a traditional comic spirit which, by jest and homely behavior, fulfilled, through the agency of make-believe, either symbolic or real actions that they would like to have performed themselves had they but dared. Toby was their Don Quixote, their knight in bib overalls. His capers against social injustices and his support of regional grievances, which to them were real indeed, gave vicarious satisfaction and thereby created a bond between them and their comic hero. The bond lasted as long as the need. When tent show dramas lost relevance for rural audiences, and when the Toby character became so exaggerated as to lose identity with them, when issues and comic hero were no longer recognizable, Toby, and the tent show along with him, fell into decline.

As a stock character, Toby possessed three important traits: his name, his red hair, and his rustic origins, all of which are identifiable with traditional comedy. From 1911 until the present, most Toby comics used the name "Toby" for all silly kid roles; and in so doing became so associated with the name that it remained with them off the stage as well. Similarly, most Toby comics wore red wigs; or, as in the case of Fred Wilson and a few others, used their own naturally red hair. And since Toby was appealing to a rural audience, and since his theatrical heritage was bucolic in nature, throughout his years of popularity he never strayed far from the farm.

The essence of Toby has always been a part of folk comedy. Early Greek comedies frequently included a "boaster" (in advance of the Roman *miles gloriosus*) and a "fool," the latter usually rustic in origin. Toby is the combination of both. The ancient playwright, Epicharmus, left us a significant title but little else in *Agrostinos, the Rustic*. However, we know a second play, *Alkyoneus*, contained a herdsman by the name of Diomos; and although the extant fragments give no clues to the nature of these exaggerated burlesques, they are believed to have treated heroic characters in contrast to those of everyday life where, according to Nicoll, the "rustic would cause laughter by his companionship with Herakles."[1] Toby, the fool of the common man, can be likened to the 15th and 16th century *Narr* of German *Fastnachtsspiel* who used an assumed stupidity to cover a native shrewdness. Sackville's Jan Bouschet, similar to the Narr, commented on or parodied the main action and, although a secondary figure, was allowed to improvise freely. Later, characters created by leading actors of the English comedians in Germany, such as John Spencer's Hans Stockfisch, Robert Reynold's Pickelherring, and eventually the natively German Hanswurst or Kasperle, utilized homespun characteristics of "clumsy ingenuousness." Ruzzanti, the bragging peasant in the farces of Angelo Beolco, was to the audiences of 16th century Italy what Toby became to the audiences of rural Illinois, Iowa, and Indiana. He took on regional dialect, and was the clown symbol of the rural underdog. The same sort of folk attachment to the fool was practiced in England where in many rural pastimes— Morris dancing, games of misrule, and jigs—the leading part can be identified as "the simple countryman, idle and roisterous in the eyes of his critics, but determined to hold his own against interfering Puritans, encroaching landlords, or the sharks and pickpurses of the city."[2] From the days of Shakespeare through the 19th century, the town and country antithesis, so popular with playwrights, kept the comic rustic alive and created prototypes of the silly kid who eventually assumed the name of Toby. Such enduring country boobies as Bottom and Quince, Dogberry and Verges, and William in *As You Like It*, have common characteristics that became a part of modern rube comedy.[3]

The low comic style used by Toby comedians was practiced in 18th century America by Thomas Wignell, making him the first low comedian of rank in the country. Wignell was the son of an actor in

Garrick's company. After Hallam had sent for Wignell, the Revolutionary War broke out, and the Hallam troupe was forced to remove to Jamaica. When the ban on theatrical performances was lifted after the war, Wignell returned with the other players and was connected with the John Street Theatre from 1785 to 1791. In no time he was established as a popular comedian with New York audiences; his portrayal of an Irish farmer turned soldier in *The Poor Soldier* and *Darby's Return* and, most significantly, of the Yankee, Jonathan, in *The Contrast* won him praise, popularity and lasting fame as the founder of rustic comedy in America.

We are indebted to William Dunlap for much of what we know about Wignell, the comic actor. From what Dunlap has written and from engravings of both *The Contrast* and *Darby's Return*, sketched by Dunlap, it is clear that Wignell was highly suitable for comic parts. Dunlap described him as

a man below the ordinary height, with a slight stoop of the shoulders; he was athletic, with handsomely formed lower extremities, the knees a little curved outwards, and feet remarkably small. His large blue eyes were rich in expression, and his comedy was luxurient in humour, but always faithful to his author. He was a comic actor not a buffoon. He was a clown who did not speak more than was set down in his part. . . . Mr. Wignell's taste was too good to permit his falling into such an error.[4]

Wignell first displayed his low comic ability in John O'Keeffe's musical farce, *The Poor Soldier*, originally performed in this country on December 2, 1785. Odell is convinced that the play, which was "overwhelmingly popular," "firmly established" Wignell's fame; he described Wignell's Darby as "unrivalled then, and always, in popular estimation."[5] Dunlap himself called the comedian "the great favorite of the laughter-loving,"[6] and suggested that his Darby "is still remembered with pleasure after a lapse of nearly half a century."[7]

The success of Wignell with Darby prompted Dunlap to write an interlude in which Darby was featured, a piece first performed during the 1789 season entitled *Darby's Return*. "This trifle," as Dunlap called it, was extremely popular for years and "several times published."[8] The first performance was made memorable by the attendance of President Washington.

The eyes of the audience were frequently bent on his countenance, and to watch the emotions produced by any particular passage upon him was the simultaneous employment of all. When Wignell, as Darby, recounts what had befallen him in America, in New York, at the adoption of the Federal Constitution, and the inauguration of the president, the interest expressed by the audience in the looks and the changes of the countenance of this great man became intense.[9]

Darby's rustic origin is expressed in a reference to the president:

> A man who fought to free the land from wo,
> *Like me*, had left his farm, a-soldiering to go;
> But having gain'd his point, he had, *like me*,
> Return'd his own potato ground to see.[10]

Dunlap's engraving of Wignell in the character of Darby shows the actor in rude dress and bushy wig taking a loutish attitude.[11] In all probability, Wignell assumed a similar appearance earlier for the Irish bumpkin in *The Poor Soldier*. A likeness between the characters of Darby and Jonathan as they were enacted by Wignell and rendered by Dunlap can be observed by comparing the drawing of Darby with Dunlap's famous sketch of the fifth act scene in *The Contrast*, rendered in 1790 for a frontispiece of a subscription printing of the play, which shows Jonathan in bushy hair and clothes closely resembling Darby's.[12] In the scene, Wignell's Jonathan behaves in typical Toby fashion. Fresh from the country, quick to aid a lady in distress, and using a language that is animated by colloquialisms and mispronunciations, Jonathan confronts the detestable Dimple with, "What the rattle ails you? Is the old one in you? Let the colonel alone, can't you? I feel chock-full of fight,—do you want to kill the colonel?" When told by the admirable Colonel Manly that Dimple does not want to harm him, Jonathan replies, "Gor! I — I wish he did; I'd shew him Yankee boys play, pretty quick. —Don't you see you have frightened the young woman into the hystrikes?"[13]

Jonathan, the first American-bred rustic, owes much to his Irish cousin, Darby. Tyler was fascinated by the theatre and was a frequent visitor behind the scenes at the John Street playhouse. He was particularly friendly with Wignell. Undoubtedly, he had seen and admired the actor's portrayal of Darby; and, enthralled by the success of the low comic action, based the character of Jonathan on this simple Irish soldier-farmer, and tailored it for the peculiar talents of the actor. The success of *The Poor Soldier*, mainly because of his skill in low comedy, must have encouraged Wignell to use the comic style of Darby in other pieces, particularly in *The Contrast* and later in *Darby's Return*. With such repetition, Wignell established rustic low comedy in America and became the father of Toby comedians.

A necessary part of Toby's paraphernalia is a wig of flaming red hair, symbolizing the demonic nature of low comedy. It is only coincidental that Fred Wilson, the father of the modern Toby, was a natural redhead; for the "crown of red hair" has been associated with comedy since Classic times when it was attached to the acting masks. In 18th century America, Wignell used a red wig for his characterizations of Darby and Jonathan. In Act III, Scene i of *The Contrast*, Jonathan describes what he has seen at a New York playhouse. The character that impressed him most—"of all the cute folk I saw, I liked one little fellow"—was Darby. Tyler and Wignell could not resist a reference to Wignell's popular creation. Jonathan identifies himself with Darby, which must have drawn pleasing audience response, as he says, "Why, he had red hair, and a little round plump face like mine, only not altogether so handsome."[14] The red wig was used by succeeding Yankee comedians as well; often directions in playbooks gave mention to their appearance in "red wig, bell-shaped hat, and striped coat and trousers."[15]

Along with the red wig, Toby's name is traditionally associated with rustic low comedy. He was an oafish country boy in Thomas Durfey's 17th century farce, *Madame Fickle* (1676), in which he and his brother, Zechiel, committed various extremes of slapstick. And as late as 1703, a short piece, *Toby and Ezekiel*, was performed at Bartholomew Fair. Previously, the farcical country manners of Shakespeare's Sir Toby Belch had evoked laughter from Elizabethan yardlings.[16] But of particular importance are Toby Allspice and Toby Twinkle, because of their appeal to 19th century comedians and their popularity with 19th century audiences.

An early comedy by Thomas Morton, *The Way to Get Married*, contains a typical country type, Toby Allspice, who is a shopkeeper, sheriff and man of lower means. He is simple enough to have been fleeced out of a thousand pounds, but shrewd enough to enforce its return. Mrs. Inchbald recalled that the play was "not merely well received" in London, "but had attraction for a considerable number of nights."[17] The piece was popular in America as well, being performed as early as 1797 at the John Street Theatre in New York. The first Joseph Jefferson was cast as Allspice, a role that remained in his repertoire for over a dozen years. The play opened the new Wallack's Lyceum in September of 1852; and it was at Wallack's that it received what was probably the last performance by a major company in this country when it was included in a series of revivals in 1862.

A second Morton play (Thomas and J. Maddison Morton) first presented at the Olympic Theatre, London, on January 13, 1851, *All That Glitters Is Not Gold, or The Poor Girl's Diary*, has in the cast a Toby Twinkle, described as "a wag employed at the mill." He is a person of lesser status, a friend of the male lead, behaving in a sympathetic but ludicrous manner, and using a humorous pattern of speech. Twinkle's first entrance in *All That Glitters* is characteristic of tent show low comedy. He has just had his nose broken in a fight defending the honor of a woman. As he backs into the room, "sparring and hitting out violently with both hands," he exclaims, "Come on! one at a time, or all at once—it's the same to me—ugh! cowards!"[18] An American production of *All That Glitters* on March 7, 1851, with Davidge as Toby Twinkle, marked the beginning of a series of presentations of the piece that lasted for over twenty years. Odell, in referring to the original performance at the Broadway Theatre, commented that, "*All That Glitters Is Not Gold* was a proverb that, before long, several New York theatres were trying to prove by means of this very play." He observed further that the play was "too good to be shelved." In the same year (1851) both Brougham and George L. Fox played Twinkle. In 1858 the role was taken by Joseph Jefferson at Laura Keene's New Theatre; and ten years later McKee Rankin performed it at the Theatre Comique. With such illustrious comedians in the part, it is apparent that in its day the comic values in the character of Toby Twinkle were worthy of the talents of the country's most able actors. By 1875, in reference to a revival at Wood's Museum, Odell was calling the piece a "favorite old play."[19] And shortly thereafter, Toby Twinkle and company passed into the hands of minor touring troupes.

The popularity of both *The Way to Get Married* and *All That Glitters Is Not Gold*, with their important comedy roles of Toby Allspice and Toby Twinkle, suggests that both pieces contributed toward the establishment of Toby as a name synonymous with low comedy. Both pieces were favorites of the country's best comedians. Both pieces enjoyed repeated revival on New York stages; and, undoubtedly, both were given a continued playing life by provincial companies.

A more recent use of the name of Toby was in Ernest C. Lamson's *Young Tobe Hoxie.* In this rural comedy-drama Tobe is a diamond-in-the-rough rustic, but not a silly kid or low comedy part. *Dramatic Compositions Coyprighted in the United States* lists the copyright date as 1900; but an 1898 recording of another Lamson title, *Mouse-trap Toby*, indicates that there was an earlier version of the piece,[20] for in *Young Tobe Hoxie*, Tobe lays plans for building a mouse trap factory.[21] The play was part of the Morey Stock Company repertoire in 1907, and was toured as late as 1909 when a Milwaukee paper carried the comment: "All the horse-play and caricature into which the pseudo-bucolic drama of the time has degenerated has been carefully eschewed by this playwright, he has revived the simple, quiet, natural depictment of country life, and its infusion with human nature, spontaneous humor and unobtrusive sympathy."[22] It should be noted in passing that the names Tobe Hoxie and Tobe Haxto of *Clouds and Sunshine* bear strong similarity.

The "silly kid" of rural dramas acquired the lasting name of Toby on the Horace Murphy tent show while Fred Wilson was engaged as light comedian: this much of the Toby controversy is acceptable to everyone. Just when the idea to call all "silly kids" by the same name was proposed and who proposed it, as well as what play served as the inspiration for the idea, are particulars that have been frequently debated by people interested in tent show lore. Since one of the principals, Fred Wilson, is no longer living, and the other, Horace Murphy, is in his eighties at this writing and cannot recall precisely what occurred, the Toby issue will never be settled to the satisfaction of everyone.

An article in *Theatre Arts* by Robert Downing[23] was probably responsible for the contemporary interest in Toby as a stock character.

The generally accepted theory is expressed in Downing's article, taken from the author's interview with Fred Wilson.[24] Downing stated that while Murphy's Comedians was playing an engagement in Crawley, La., in 1909, Murphy and Wilson were approached by a ten year old boy. The lad expressed his confusion that Wilson had portrayed Tobe Haxton in *Clouds and Sunshine* on Monday night, Toby Green in *Out of the Fold* on Tuesday night, and Bud in *Won by Waiting* on Wednesday night. Why, the boy questioned, since Wilson looked, dressed, and talked the same in all three roles did he call himself Bud in the Wednesday night play, and Toby in the other two? Downing suggests Murphy's reaction to the discovered inconsistency by the following assumption: "That season, he and Wilson applied Toby's name to all silly-kid parts in their repertory. The idea spread rapidly to other managements, and Toby was born."[25] Clark and Snyder differ from Downing in only a few details. Calling Downing's statement the "authentic version" of Toby's origin, Clark adds that "showmen generally agree" that *Clouds and Sunshine* was used by Murphy in 1909 and that Wilson played the role of Tobe. Further, Clark credits W. C. Herman with writing the first play "in which the 'country boy' character was called Toby."[26] In addition to presenting material from Downing's article, Snyder includes statements from Fred Wilson's widow, Pearle Wilson Nicholson, obtained from an interview in 1958. Mrs. Nicholson told Snyder that Toby originated in Crowley, La., on the Murphy show in 1909.[27] When confronted by the questioning boy, Wilson "was struck with the idea of calling all of his characterizations 'Toby'."[28]

Dr. Mickel, who is a good deal more knowledgeable on the subject than either Clark or Snyder, and whose contributions to tent show research are considerable, is in general agreement with all three writers. He sums up his views in the following:

Acting on this hint, Murphy gave Wilson instructions to convert all the "first comedy" parts in their shows to the Toby character. Tobe Haxton of *Clouds and Sunshine*, whose first name easily and naturally shifts to Toby, must therefore be considered the first to emerge as Toby himself.[29]

Mickel adds that when Byers of the Chicago Manuscript Company was informed of the success Wilson was enjoying in his Toby roles, he ordered the playwrights in his employ to turn out pieces that included a Toby character.[30]

Neil Schaffner's explanation of the affair is more varied and undoubtedly more apocryphal than the others. Schaffner writes that in 1912 he was a light comedian for a stock company in Fort Dodge, Iowa. During that engagement a copy of *Clouds and Sunshine* was submitted to director Lorin H. Guin by Alex Byers; and a short time later the play was performed by the company. Inspired by the unexpected success of the play, and pleased with the audience acceptance of Tobe Haxton as played by Schaffner, Guin wrote Byers a letter of affirmation, commenting particularly on the role of Tobe. Schaffner attests further that

Byers sent the script, together with Guin's testimonial to Horace Murphy, who then had two repertoire companies playing in tents in Louisiana under the name of Murphy's Comedians. Murphy sent it to his No. 2 unit where a young, red-headed actor named Fred Wilson was the comedian.[31]

After giving the play a public sampling, Wilson, according to Schaffner, found it to be such an audience pleaser that he used it as an opening bill in the next town. The second night's attraction was *Won by Waiting*, in which the light comedy part of Bud is mentioned several times before the character actually appears. Eventually, the character woman goes to the door and calls out, "Bud! Bud! You come right in here!" On this particular evening, as Wilson entered, a small boy seated in the front of the house called out, "Heck, that ain't Bud, that's To-be!" With this, Wilson stepped forward and retorted, "You're right, son, I *am* Tobe, and from now on everybody is going to call me that." Several days later, when Murphy paid a visit to his No. 2 show, he was informed of the incident; thereon "he immediately decided that from then on all rube characters in plays presented by Murphy's Comedians would be called Tobe."[32]

Important to the explanation of Toby's origin are 1) the year, 2) the place, 3) the manner in which it came about, 4) the men responsible for the decision, and 5) the play that inspired the action. There is no doubt that the men instrumental in the birth of Toby were Horace Murphy and Fred Wilson; all of the aforementioned agree, although in one case it is implied that Schaffner was the first to perform a Toby role. Downing's suggestion that Crawley, La., was the scene for the important decision is correct, except for a misspelling. Mickel is inclined to accept Lafayette, La., which he has taken from Robert L. Sherman's *Drama Cyclopedia* on the basis that no Crawley is listed as a Louisiana town.[33] There is, however, a Crowley, La., and Murphy has confirmed that this was the town in question.[34] The year was neither 1909 nor 1912; that it was 1911 will be explained later. The play was not *Clouds and Sunshine* but *Out of the Fold*. And, if the incident with the small boy is fact, it was not recalled by Horace Murphy when this writer interviewed him in 1967.

By the time Murphy was using *Out of the Fold*, the play had been performed around the country for several years. The New York debut occurred on March 7, 1904 at the American Theatre at 42nd Street between Seventh and Eighth Avenues. The leading roles were taken by Theodore Babcock, Sylvia Bidwell, and author Langdon McCormick. Toby Tompkins was played by George Fox.[35] The New York run lasted for three weeks, or a total of twenty-four performances. The play was thereafter toured to principal cities of the East: Newark, Philadelphia, Providence, Brooklyn, Jersey City, and back to New York for a week at the Metropolis Theatre.[36]

At least three Chicago theatres presented McCormick's play. Prior to the New York opening, beginning June 21, 1903, the play was staged at the Great Northern Theatre, billed as a "new melodrama."[37] When in August of 1904 the play was repeated at the Alhambra Theatre, Dan MacMillan was said to be "hugely funny" as the "pudgy moonfaced schoolboy."[38] And the following year the Players Stock Company at the Bush Temple was "so far superior to the rendition of the same nice, chunky, village gossip tragedy at the Great Northern, that the first showing of the play cannot be compared to this last."[39]

McCormick's play was undoubtedly a favorite with many of the stock companies across the country. Boston audiences were entertained by it in April of 1908 at the Castle Square Theatre with Louis Albion as Toby.[40] The Boyle Stock Company, playing at the Grand in Nashville, Tenn., in the autumn of 1904, featured the Toby of Donald Meek, who had recently joined the company. He was described by a writer for the Nashville *American* as being "one of the hits of the evening."[41] And the company at the Shubert Theatre, Milwaukee, gave the piece a week's run in April of 1909.[42] It is apparent, then, that *Out of the Fold* was a popular and proven rural drama and that Toby Tompkins had been the bucolic creation of many a stock company comedian by the time Horace Murphy and Fred Wilson discovered it and turned it into an important part of tent show history.

Murphy's account of how Toby Tompkins became Toby, the stock character of tent show comedy-drama, as told to this writer in two taping sessions, is as follows: In 1910 Horace Murphy purchased a used tent and began a lengthy career as a tent show manager. As he stated it, he left a job on the Cotton Blossom Show Boat "to get away from the river because I wanted to branch out." His first stand was in Baton Rouge, where he opened with *In Old Kentucky*, and "gave 'em a hell of a good performance of it."[43] In the early part of the 1911 season Murphy's Comedians was playing in Illinois. A *Billboard* item places the company in Sparta, Illinois, on June 15, 1911, where the show was doing well in a new tent, playing small towns "in and about" the state. It was disclosed that the 25-people organization was set for a tour of the South and Southeast for the remainder of the summer.[44] It was while the company was in Illinois that Wilson left a stock job and joined the tent show, a move that was to strengthen Murphy's acting troupe.

Wilson was not only the first comedian to call himself Toby in all the rube roles he played, he was perhaps the best Toby comedian of all time. Tent show manager Ed. L. Copeland has described him as being born with red hair and a snub nose. Further,

His gait and posture are unassumed, and he was fortunate or unfortunate enough to lose just enough teeth to make his mouth the envy of any "Toby" comedian, and his way of putting it over is an art seldom seen in a character of this kind.

Copeland, writing in 1920, judged Wilson to be "the cleverest kid comedian I have ever had the pleasure of meeting."[45] Murphy is generous in his admiration of Wilson, both as a man and as an actor. "Boy, he was a great comedian! . . . Wilson had a lot of good specialties; he not only was a good comedian." In describing his natural approach to a role, Murphy stated:

And he didn't act a bit. He just said the words and let 'em come out; but they were so doggoned natural it reminded everybody of themselves. . . . He did refined hokum. He did hokum that you see in your home. . . . I used to think I was a good Toby when I was young because I got a lot of laughs; but I had to stretch a point here and there to get the laughs. Toby could sit down and get 'em.[4]

The performance that inspired the idea of calling all rube silly kids Toby occurred, as nearly as can be estimated, sometime in the summer of 1911, before there were more than one Murphy's Comedians on the road. Murphy had been on a trip to New York, leaving Wilson in charge of the company. During his absence, *Out of the Fold* must have been added to the repertoire. Murphy has described his rejoining in Crowley, La., in these words: "And the night I got in there they put on this *Out of the Fold* and it made such an impression with me."

Thereafter, he continued, "we made everything a Toby except *Rip Van Winkle* and we couldn't find a spot."47

"They were all wrong about the way it started," Murphy said. His responses to the kid on the street story was "Well, that's all the bunk! . . . When I wrote Wilson, when I got this thing here (referring to the Downing article), what the hell do you mean telling this reporter this misconception of how Toby was originated? You know that I sat down after that show and talked it over and decided to change all them to Tobys. Why bring in some little, innocent kid on the street? He wrote back and said, 'I didn't do it; the guy either misunderstood me or he took a lot of liberties or something!' "48

Included in the repertoire at the time were *Thorns and Orange Blossoms*, *Rip Van Winkle*, and *St. Elmo*, traditional pieces outside the mold of rural dramas. But Murphy vowed that "every comedy part we got in every play is going to be called Toby." In *Thorns and Orange Blossoms*, the light comedy part was not a rube, but a person who mingled with royalty; so Toby was made a guide on a hunting expedition by an English Lord visiting America.49

There can be little doubt about *Out of the Fold* being performed by Wilson before *Clouds and Sunshine*. In the first place, *Out of the Fold* was copyrighted in 1902, *Clouds and Sunshine* in 1911. Murphy declared he had not heard of *Clouds and Sunshine* until he had played *Out of the Fold* "for quite a while."

It seems to me we played this first (*Out of the Fold*) and Alex Byers, whom Herman was writing for at the time, found out about it. . . . It seems to me I wrote him about this Toby thing in *Out of the Fold* . . . but it might have been Herman that I wrote.50

In all likelihood, *Clouds and Sunshine* was written by Herman sometime after the success of Fred Wilson in *Out of the Fold*. Retired actor B. E. Walton recalled that the former was staged as a "trial run" on the G. Carlton Guy show while the company was playing in theatres. Since it was after the tenting season, Walton assumes the time of initial performance to be either the autumn of 1911 or early 1912; in any case, it was before the piece was copyrighted and sold to Alex Byers. However, Walton's recollections are too uncertain to be of any real help.

I'm pretty certain that Cal wrote *Clouds and Sunshine* in 1911 since he came on the Guy show after I had spent one summer on the show. It is possible that Cal came on for the winter season of 1911 and wrote his play the next year, but I'm not sure. I do know that we ran a premier of his play in perhaps Muncie or Kokomo, Ind., just a one nighter and I recall Guy posting someone in the rear of the theatre to call out "AUTHOR!" "AUTHOR!" I recall old Cal taking his bow and we all were very proud of him.[51]

Walton is confused about the copyright status of the play during the "trial run;" *Clouds and Sunshine* was copyrighted by Alex Byers on September 5, 1911.[52]

The two plays show a similarity of plot. *Out of the Fold* is concerned with the dilemma of Helene Grey, a city girl with an erring past who has come to a small town to expiate her sins by leading a good life. She takes a job as assistant to Nolan Crane, a young schoolmaster. The two fall in love and are about to be married when a former friend of Crane's, John Lathrop, interferes by exposing Miss Grey's past. Lathrop, while in the city attending college, had been in love with her. Crane publicly defends his fiancée, but torn between his love and social conventions, vows he will not marry. The nasty situation is helped along by village gossips. Ultimately, however, the two lovers are united, Crane retains the teaching appointment he was on the verge of resigning, and the villainous Lathrop is soundly rejected. The play's comic relief is supplied primarily by a young country boy with a large appetite, Toby Tompkins, and his "tom boy" sister, Suzanne. In *Clouds and Sunshine* the heroine is a school teacher, Marjorie Morgan, who, because she refused to divulge her past to the school board president after discouraging his affectionate advances, is turned out of the boarding house where she has been residing and threatened with discharge from her teaching job. She is taken into the home of a wealthy minister when all other doors are closed to her. The two fall in love. But when the minister's reprobate brother, who has been living in the city, exposes Marjorie Morgan as a married woman, Reverend Joe Tucker calls off his intended marriage to her, and lays plans to resign from his position with the church. Here, too, village gossips play a role in disparaging Miss Morgan. Eventually, the husband turns up, is done in by the black sheep brother over money matters, and the minister and the school teacher are united. The young comedy roles, Tobe Haxton and Susie Green, are much like the Toby and Suzanne of *Out of the Fold*, although they are not brother and sister. In fact, the similarity of plot and characters between these plays leads one to suspect that Herman borrowed more from *Out of the Fold* than Fred Wilson's Toby.

In summary, with the facts available to this writer, the following account can be given: Murphy's Comedians was organized in 1910 in Louisiana. By the spring of 1911 the company had worked its way to Illinois where it remained until late June. During the stay in Illinois, Fred Wilson joined the cast. Shortly thereafter, Murphy left for New York, leaving Wilson in charge. On his return, Murphy was impressed with the comic character of Toby Tompkins, as played by Fred Wilson. That very evening they talked about the role and decided to try using the name Toby for all of the rube kids that Wilson was portraying. So intent were they in this plan that they not only changed the names of the characters, but re-wrote the plays to accommodate a silly kid. Moreover, Murphy told Alex Byers or Cal Herman or someone else connected with the Chicago Manuscript Company of his success with *Out of the Fold*. With this knowledge, Herman immediately turned out *Clouds and Sunshine* in the mold of McCormick's play, with Byers copyrighting it in September of 1911. The acclaim Wilson received as Toby led others to follow his practice; soon there were many tent shows featuring Toby comedians and performing an entire repertoire of Toby bills.

CHAPTER IX. TENT SHOW OPERATIONAL PRACTICES

OPERATIONAL PATTERNS DEVELOPED DURING THE FLURRY OF ROAD activity by repertoire and one-night stand companies throughout the last quarter of the 19th century were combined with those of the American circus, as opera house physical characteristics were placed into the portable circus tent, to form the theatrical structure of the repertoire tent show. Consequently, repertoire proprietors were faced with added business responsibilities as they became both company manager and theatre owner.

Opera house repertoire companies toured with a modicum of scenery, some advertising paper, and trunks of the actors; tent shows, on the other hand, carried a larger stock of scenery, more paper, and all of the necessary equipment to construct and transport a portable theatre. Except for some southern shows that performed year around, a tenting season lasted eighteen to twenty-five weeks, or from mid-spring until the weather became too cold to attract audiences in the fall. This could be extended by winterizing the tent. Coke burning stoves made out of steel drums, called salamanders, gave out heat without creating smoke; and if the tent was insulated with a second layer of sidewall, the salamanders were efficient in diminishing early winter chill.

When weather forced a company to close, the equipment was stored at what circuses called winter quarters. Most shows wintered in small communities where real estate could be purchased or leased cheaply, where taxes were insignificant, and where there was less danger of vandalism and theft. The Kelly Stock Company, for example, stored in Laingsburg, Michigan, since Jack Kelly's home was in Lansing, a large community a few miles distant.[1] At winter quarters the necessary building, repairing, and painting was done to prepare for re-opening in the spring, for showmen were proud of their outfits and made every effort to keep them attractive.

A crew of men experienced in working with tents was a necessary part of a manager's salary list. This meant hiring anywhere from five to a dozen tent hands each season. Frequently, the band boys doubled on canvas. And with small shows, actors were required to perform certain duties in putting up and taking down the tent. This undertaking did not appeal to all dramatic artists, as is illustrated by an irate complaint to the *Billboard* that "when anyone with histrionic ability in this system joins a repertoire show under canvas, he may not anticipate that in addition to his 'acting out,' the manager may have so little regard for an 'akter's artistic temperament' as to expect the newcomer to 'work on canvas'—in other words, to be a canvasman on the side."[2] In reply, Frank J. Doherty listed several companies with which he had been associated that did not require actors to double canvas: Rentfrow Stock Company, Chase-Lister, Grandi Stock Company, Jack Raymond Company, Park Stock Company, Elwin Strong Players, Harrison Stock Company, Guy Players, and W. I. Swain. These companies carried between twenty-five and forty people; in only rare instances did any of the actors even double band and orchestra. According to manager W. I. Swain, his performers had specific instructions to stay off the show lot until work was finished. Overseeing the working men was a canvas specialist, the boss canvasman. Such a person was Jack Hunt of the Barnum and Bailey Circus. "A few years ago Jack was himself a member of the common working gang," a writer commented in 1895, "working for four dollars and a half a week; but ability tells in putting up tents as in other things, and now he holds one of the most important positions in this most perfectly organized of all armies, the modern circus."[3] Canvas was always vulnerable to the elements. The boss canvasman who knew his job could save a tent from the frequently destructive storms encountered throughout a season. Many of these were men schooled in the frenetic operational system of the circus who preferred the less harried week stands to the one-day-in-a-town routine.

The greatest fear of show people, damage to equipment by fire, was a particular menace because it struck without warning; and the waterproofing compound used prior to World War II, naphtha and paraffin, caused the canvas to burn with unbelievable rapidity. A carelessly thrown cigarette could mean total loss of a tent outfit. A few examples suggest innumerable occurrences. The Melville Comedians suffered a fire of unknown origin in Little Rock in 1915, with an estimated loss of between $7,000 and $8,000. The conflagration of Bert Melville's canvas theatre, "which destroyed his life's work," lasted twenty minutes, for the tent had recently been waterproofed. The same year, Angell's Comedians, managed by Ed C. Nutt, lost everything except wardrobe and a few properties in Oakdale, La., when the outfit caught fire from a nearby burning building. Two years later the same company, then managed by Billy Angelo, lost the entire outfit in Benton, Arkansas after a carelessly thrown match ignited the recently paraffined sidewall. In 1916 the Haverstock Stock Company suffered damage in Olney, Texas; the company's baggage car burned while loaded with the entire show. The Ed C. Nutt Comedy Company was destroyed in LaFayette, La., in 1917 when fire broke out shortly after the matinee. Everything was lost except some of the actors' wardrobe. Two years later, in Clinton, Ind., John Lawrence's tent burned to the ground from what was thought to have been a cigarette thrown onto the tent by town boys. The 80-foot top was valued at $1,800 and the scenery at over $2,000. A cigarette caused a $5,000 loss for J. Doug Morgan in 1920 while his troupe was playing in Sulphur Springs, Texas. The incident occurred only fifteen minutes before matinee time; but, miraculously, no one was harmed. It is interesting to note that in most cases these companies did not close; adversity was part of the barnstorming tradition. In Melville's case, the local Kempner Theatre was booked for the remainder of the stay. A new tent was ordered within a half hour after the fire. In like manner, Haverstock immediately ordered a new outfit which was assembled while the company continued in opera houses.

Storms were also a common danger to the tent nomad. Managers expected a number of days of bad weather each year and prepared for cyclonic winds in advance. A good tent man could almost smell the approach of a storm. He braced against it by double-staking the critical spots around the tent, adding belly ropes over the top to keep the canvas from billowing, securing heavy center poles at their base to prevent them from dancing, and pulling the guy lines tight to lessen the danger of ropes breaking. But even with these precautions, storms took their toll. Manager Charles Wortham experienced many blowdowns in his central Illinois territory; on one occasion, a violent wind scattered pieces of the tent three and four miles over the countryside. When wind struck Doc Rucker's tent show in northwestern Ohio, everything was flattened in "a twinkling of an eye;" although the storm occurred in mid-afternoon, the tent was mended and set back up in time for the evening performance. The Herbert-Gilpin Stock Company was hit by a tornado one evening, which blew the tent away, leaving "a scared and unhurt audience waiting for the show." A new tent was ordered at once; and the replacement happened so quickly that only one night was lost. Billy Bennett was not so fortunate. When a cyclone struck in Parham, Minn., at show time, the tent collapsed burying the audience beneath. Overturned lights caused a fire and many of the people were badly burned. Playing in Fargo, Okla., the Blondin Stock Company tent was completely blown away. The following day a farmer living three miles from town brought in a piece of the canvas with Blondin's name on it. With a flair of showmanship, Blondin scribbled a lifetime ticket on the tattered canvas and returned it to the farmer. As with fire, few performances were lost; if violent storms left the canvas top unserviceable, the canvas sidewall was erected around the seating in airdome fashion, permitting the show to take place under the open sky.

As the popularity of tented drama increased, enterprising managers found it profitable to place more than one show on the road. For example, Jack Kelly was the proprietor of two Michigan shows known as Kelly Stock Company No. 1, and Kelly Stock Company No 2. There was a limit to the amount of expansion that a single show could undergo. Once a seating capacity had been stretched to 1,500 or 2,000, a larger tent was impractical in terms of sight and sound. No. 2 shows were frequently formed from cast-off equipment from the original company. Since secondhand show property sold for only a fraction of its initial cost and less than its actual worth, it was feasible, when a tent was replaced and an outfit refurbished, to make use of the old equipment by putting out a No. 2 show. With good fortune, a summer's profit might allow the second company to improve and replace shabby equipment. Finally, two companies operating a mutual territory under a single management tended to discourage opposition from other shows; the ability to move them about like chessmen served as an effective weapon against interlopers. For these and other reasons, such established show names as Gordinier Brothers, Chase-Lister Stock Company, Angell's Comedians, Ed. C. Nutt Stock Company, and Fred Brunk's Comedians found it advantageous to place No. 2 companies on the road.

Such expansion was not limited to two units. Two years after the Brunk Brothers had added a second company, they were operating four. The manager of one of the outfits was Harley Sadler, who later owned one of the largest and most successful tent repertoires to play the state of Texas. Roy E. Fox, who was said to have financial interest in several Texas shows, announced in 1917 the formation of a second company and indicated plans for putting out more during the season. The Dubinsky Brothers had as many as ten shows operating at one time in the Central States. Horace Murphy, who entered repertoire management in 1910, had six companies by 1914. His initial success was so great, touring through what he called Louisiana's "death valley," that he tried to book all of his companies on an identical route, playing each town at two week intervals. He found, however, that this system did not work; for, in his words, "First man there kills the other fellow." The original company to perform in a town had the advantage of being the first to gain public recognition and support; companies that followed were looked on as inferior or mere imitations.

Expansion of holdings by repertoire managers just prior to and during World War I suggests the degree of prosperity enjoyed by tent showmen throughout this period. The fertile show territories of the Middlewest and South soon became overrun with dramatic tent shows, a condition that created strong rivalries between companies for "ownership" of the better towns. This was apparent as early as 1914 when manager W. I. Swain reported that the past tenting season had shown increased opposition from other shows. It was not unusual for the average size midwestern community to accommodate as many as five week-stand tent shows in a single summer. This crowded situation lasted throughout the golden age of tent repertoire and ended with the Wall Street disaster of 1929. Good show towns were hard to come by and could mean the difference between a winning and losing season. With the intrusion of other companies, there was the danger of a town being theatrically over-worked. Several shows playing and taking money out of a town in a single summer affected the local economy. Local disapprobation could result in tent shows being barred from the community through the enactment of exhorbitant license fees. It is not surprising then that managers were highly protective of their territories.

Arranging routes sometimes resembled a chess game. Once when Angell's Comedians advertised to play one of W. I. Swain's towns, the flamboyant Swain cancelled a previous booking to go into the town a week before the rival company, forcing the Angell advance man to switch to another community, one that had been played by the Swain show four weeks earlier.[4] Occasionally, two companies played the same town on the same week. This was called a day-and-date. Ermin Gray was a performer with Gabe Garrett's Comedians at a time when the show day-and-dated rival Fred Brunk's Comedians, with outfits set up back-to-back, only separated by an alley. Gray recalls that both shows, competing to the very end, opened their stand with the same play, *The Awakening of John Slater*.[5] Neil Schaffner told of the rivalry between J. Doug Morgan and Hila Morgan for Iowa towns. Hila was the widow of Doug's brother, Fred. Before his death Fred had been an outstanding advance man and promoter and had made "a great deal of money." Hila, who billed herself as "Iowa's Little Sweetheart," felt that Doug was "trying to put her out of business." This enmity resulted in a struggle over towns. According to Schaffner, Hila began playing Doug's towns ahead of him and using other tactics such as covering his paper with banners reading, "Wait for Hila!" Most managers were able to cope with the competition more rationally. For example, in 1924 managers Lloyd T. Gould and George Lanshaw, both operating Michigan companies with overlapping territories, met in Robert J. Sherman's office in Chicago to mutually arrange their summer itineraries, "selecting and swapping towns for the good of business." Like children dividing candy, the managers bargained "by the old you-take-this-one-and-I'll-take-that-one method." Considerations included such things as who would play certain prize towns first and the number of weeks that should properly elapse before the next show came in. If engagements were spaced to allow a period of theatrical calm within a community, the local motion picture theatre manager was less apt to be antagonistic toward visiting tent shows.

As a consequence he is not always appealing to the town council to raise the license. The local showgoers are not fed up with fourteen to twenty straight days of tent repertory and it gives them a chance to appreciate both shows.[7]

It should be understood that the use of questionable competitive methods mentioned here was not commonly practiced. For the most part, there was a friendly and co-operative relationship between companies, as well as a feeling of understanding and comradeship that is usual with groups involved in similar pursuits.

A local opera house manager conducting a seasonal operation used a routine system of advertising that varied little from week to week; but a tent show manager who booked each town only once a year did not enjoy that kind of continuity. Neither could tent shows afford to build attendance throughout the week; they needed large houses from the opening night. Many advertising methods of the repertoire tent shows, particularly the heavy emphasis on printed material such as lithographs, cards, and handbills, and the flamboyant manner in which such material was applied, were borrowed directly from the circus. "Billing like a circus!" was the boast of many a tent show advance man. Colorful one-sheet lithographs were pasted on barns, fences, and billboards, daubed side by side, as many as it took to fill the available space, always enlivened with ink of red and blue to create the desired flash.

The circus was the first to use billboard type advertising. In the early days, an advance man left placards at conspicuous locations. He was followed by a bugler on horseback, heralding the approach of the troupe. When the show left town the placards posted in such places as livery stables, taverns, and post offices were usually torn down to be used again and again. Until 1849 posters were printed with black ink; then R. Sands & Co.'s Hippoferaean Arena used a color display of two elephants hitched to "the East Indian Car," and Crane & Co.'s Great Oriental Circus used a two-color poster depicting "the Great Eyptian Dragon Chariot." The usual lithograph found in front of theatres at the turn of the century was called a one-sheet. As the largest single sheet that could be printed on the old hand presses, it became a standard measurement among billposters. As circuses grew in size and number, making it necessary to increase advertising efforts, circus managers reasoned that if a one-sheet in black and white was effective, then a larger spread in various colors would prove even more so. By 1896 a 42-sheet stand in six or seven colors was not an unusual sight. This kind of flash advertising was adopted by repertoire tent shows. The Brenner-Nixon-Brown Company was not unique in billing their towns within a twenty mile radius. One year the Kelly Stock Company boasted that in a single season its advance agent (Dave Heilman) traveled 7,682 miles and used nearly 10,000 sheets of paper.

Following the practice of both the circus and the opera house companies, tent shows used an advance man whose job it was to travel a week ahead. He secured show lots, preferably in the center of town, easily accessible to all. He paid city licenses required for traveling entertainments. (Sometimes there was a county license to be paid as well.) He saw to it that handbills were distributed by local town boys and were mailed to rural areas by local post offices. He placed advertising and free readers with newspapers. Some agents (as the advance men were sometimes called) were allowed to determine the show's routing. This required a familiarity with the territory. Which communities are traditionally good "show towns?" What time of the year are they most receptive to traveling entertainment? What time of the month is the working man's payday? When are the crops harvested? For example, during cotton picking time in Arkansas and Texas, field hands were paid daily; therefore, it was preferable to play the cotton country at the harvesting. A good advance man was worth more than his salary. Since a good opening was half of the battle in week repertoire, he was sometimes allowed a percentage of the opening night receipts as an incentive.

A concert band, originally used exclusively by circuses but later adopted by many types of touring attractions, served as an outstanding means of publicity. The circus of Purdy and Welch, operating before 1835, may have been the first to carry a band and conduct a parade. Earlier circuses used merely drums and fifes. In the golden age of the circus, bands were so popular they were featured in newspaper and billboard advertising. Large circuses included marching bands in their parades. Smaller shows that did not parade gave band concerts at main intersections and in front of the tent before show time. Many tent show people broke into the profession as bandmen. For example, M. A. Hunt, manager of the Hunt Stock Company, a Michigan tent show, was a member of the rube band with Frank Tucker's house repertoire company for several years before he went into business for himself. Horace Murphy was a boy tiple-tongue cornetist, performing with everything from medicine shows to showboats, prior to forming Murphy's Comedians.[8] Since bands were the public's measure of a show's worth, every effort was made to enhance the spectacle of the band concerts. The size of the band was impressive to potential patrons; so actors were frequently handed corked instruments and required to fake playing them. Ben Wilkes, who toured through southern Illinois in the '20's, used his band as a special feature of the show. Wilkes played cornet and his wife the trombone. A concert was given every noon in the town square and at four and seven o'clock the band was driven through town on a truck. In the middle of each concert Wilkes would remove his hat and offer a pitch for the night's performance, always including the phrase, "Nothing said or done to harm the most fastidious!" When Mason Wilkes (no relation) joined the show in the mid-twenties, he was handed a "peck horn" (alto) and told to stand in. During his first concert he heard a youngster shout repeatedly, "He's not playing! He's not playing!" The incident caused Mason such embarrassment that he immediately started learning the instrument.[9] The value of a band to tent shows was indicated in a 1906 *Billboard* editorial: "All things being equal" recent statistics show that repertoire shows carrying bands "have done much better business than those that have not carried bands."[10]

Another advertising device taken from the circus was the steam calliope, a musical organ that operated either manually or by music rolls. Invented by William Hoyt of Dupont, Ind., it was first put to commercial use by Joshua C. Stoddard for a political excursion on the Boston and Main Railroad in 1856. Stoddard described his organ as a "New Musical Instrument to be Played by the Agency of Steam or Highly Compressed Air." Circus publicity men made quick use of the unique machine to enhance the spectacle of the parade. In 1857 Nixon and Kemp advertised it as a "robust music maker, belching steam and smoke." After the instruments became powered by gasoline engines more compact and efficient than steam, repertoire companies began to use them. In 1916 the Allmann Comedy Company announced that a large calliope had been recently purchased to be featured along with the band in "uptown concerts." Eventually, the calliope replaced the band altogether, and mounted on a truck, it was driven around town pumping soulful tunes, calling attention to the advertising banners displayed on the truck sideboards.

Some tent shows made use of the circus-type "free act" as a promotional stunt, arranged to bring people onto the show lot for a short program of free entertainment, the theory being that once a crowd gathered, it was a simple matter to sell everyone a ticket to the show. One season, for example, the Milton Comedy Company engaged Bell, the high-diving dog, as an attraction. What was described as "one of the most unusual features carried by any company" was displayed by Ed. C. Nutt in 1916. The act was Harry "Crazy" Rich and "his startling and wonderful feats of strength, skill, and daring."

His performances are put on daily, and for crowd-getters and breath-stoppers there are few to compare with his. Crowds begin to assemble on the street long before the free attraction is put on to get a glimpse of Rich performing many feats in the air from a high wire.[12]

Typically, small towners possessed a passion for sporting events. During the summer months baseball held their attention; the local independent team drew large crowds each Sunday afternoon. Wily tent proprietors exploited this public interest by forming ball teams from company personnel and playing the popular local organizations. The show's name lettered across the chest of its baseball players was good publicity. Often the tent was set up in a recreational park; therefore, the crowds drawn to a ball game were made aware of the show's presence. Frequently, company teams were composed of talented athletes. While W. I. Swain's tent show was set up in Piggott, Arkansas, the local ball team called on members of the company to help them defeat a team from a nearby town. The actors assisted admirably with Paul English pitching a no-hit-no-run game which included striking out seventeen batters. Ed Nutt reported in 1914 that after touring 53 weeks without a lay-off a baseball team was organized which proved "a terror to all the town teams along the way." Members of the band were often hired for their athletic ability as much as for their musical talents. Horace Murphy took great pains in selecting his bandmen to fill the nine positions on a baseball field. If a musician failed in baseball, he was given two weeks pay and his transportation home. Eventually, Murphy assembled a remarkable ballplaying band that, after the show moved to California in 1914, won 40 of 44 games. The Seven Cairns Brothers was said to have carried the most unique band and ball team on the road. All seven brothers were both musicans and baseball players; and their 1917 record of 52 wins of 70 games would indicate they were at least good on the ball field.

Although some tent show managers were actors as well, the combination was commonly unsuccessful. Many of the companies formed by actors with a desire to work for themselves and thereby receive profits far in excess of a single salary did not last long. A new tent outfit cost about $10,000. By careful purchase of used equipment, a show could be organized for somewhat less; still, the investment was sizeable in terms of an actor's pay. But men with a keen sense of survival, and strength against adversities, with insight to public response, promotional imagination, and with knowledge of good theatre practice, fashioned managerial careers that lasted for many years, until overwhelming forces of depression, war, and changing times marked the end of tent repertoire as an active rural entertainment.

COMMENTARY

IN HIS APPRAISAL OF THE PROFUSIVE NUMBER OF *UNCLE TOM'S CABIN*
companies on the road in the 19th century, Furnas commented that
these shows brought "low cost excitement and massed laughter to
places where it occasioned several hours of intense discussion when
a stranger drove past the feedstore."[1] In judging the value of the
repertoire tent show activity the same can be said. If tent shows
contributed nothing to the art of the theatre, they at least created
a mass audience for the drama. Many of today's playgoers can
recall that their first experience with live theatre occurred in a tent.
Repertoire troupes appeared under canvas in hundreds of out-of-the-
way communities where railroad house troupes never ventured, where
a full stage production was unknown to an audience accustomed to
being entertained from the back of a Hamlin's Wizard Oil Company
wagon.

The combined yearly audiences of tent shows exceeded the
annual attendance of New York theatres. *Billboard* reported more
than 300 shows operating under canvas in 1926 playing to a total
audience of over 18,000,000 people.[2] The following year the Tent
and Repertoire Managers' Protective Association advertised the existence of over 400 shows with an annual attendance of over 78,000,000

people.[3] Granted, these claims show a wide disagreement on total figures; nevertheless, since no accurate records exist, one can only assume that tent shows were seen by an impressively large number of Americans.

As tent shows created a theatre audience, they, at the same time, developed actors. The existence of some 300 or 400 companies, using at least ten dramatic performers in each, provided an enormous training opportunity for would-be professionals. It has already been pointed out that following World War I the demand for actors exceeded the available supply. Certainly, the need for performers at that time opened the way for young and untried talent, providing a learning atmosphere as useful and as boundless as any other American theatre activity. It was comparable to the old stock companies of the 19th century. The comments of Otis Skinner about his training at the Philadelphia Museum seem apt.

I learned my art crudely, roughly, but by leaps and bounds, driven by necessity to an intuitive grasp of character and the way to express it. To sing; to dance, to fence with foil and broadsword; to kneel; to fall in combat; to work up the crescendo movement of a scene; to sit or to rise; to play fair in a give-and-take episode with a fellow-player; to learn how to make up, and above all, to do nothing.[4]

By present day standards the quality of entertainment was shabby. Sets were two-dimensional, rickety, and well worn. Costumes consisted chiefly of what each actor brought in his trunk. Plays were the kite-tail of Victorian melodrama, simple, sentimental, and crudely composed. Acting was straightforward, sometimes overdone, loud, and lacking in subtleties. But, then, such criticism can be directed at even the high-class drama of that period. There is no way to assess the dramatic quality of 300 or more shows, performing in various regions of the country, and constantly moving about. There were excellently managed companies and there were those that operated under a practice of "give it to them quick and send them home." There were companies that possessed flashy street bands and jazz orchestras, but carried weak stage shows. There were companies that displayed few frills, but presented a sound, enjoyable, and even artistic program of quality actors and quality vaudeville entertainers. Unquestionably, many tent show actors were as good as those in the better New York companies. On the other hand, there were some who were primarily musicians or variety performers, but, hired to double, merely filled out the cast as best they could.

Contemporary journalists, in their enchantment with the Toby character, have tended to over-emphasize him. The ability of Neil Schaffner, one of the last of the Toby comedians, to secure space in newspapers and national magazines, did much to enhance the image of Toby in modern tent companies. From contemporary articles, it is easy to assume that the modern Toby show is typical of the tent shows of yesteryear. In truth, once Toby proved his audience appeal he was freely utilized; whenever there was a "silly kid" role, Toby was on hand. However, many of the repertoire companies used no Toby bills. For example, there was a time when competing Michigan shows—the Hunt Stock Company, Kelly Stock Company, and the Slout Players—advertised, "All Broadway Royalty Plays!" The same is true for other parts of the country. Such pieces as *Cat and the Canary, Nothing But the Truth, Twin Beds,* and *Up in Mabel's Room* were frequently representative of a company's repertoire.

It might even be suggested that Toby was in part responsible for the decline of tent shows. His strong rustic heritage expressed through the antic of low comedy did not allow tent drama to progress with changing times. The rural setting endured, since it was necessary for Toby's bucolic comedy, into the age of H-bombs, jet planes, and massive urban problems. Tent shows were unable to get off the farm. Toby further deteriorated tent show quality by his refusal to stay within the play. Exuberant Toby comedians committed all kinds of improvised tomfoolery, leaping out of character, stopping the play completely to carry on some discourse with the audience, and even running up and down the aisles. Such behavior pushed the play into secondary importance; and when the drama is lost, so are the actors and their audience. Warning against imprudent use of the ad lib and other erratic stage behavior was issued by no less authority than William Shakespeare, whose wisdom has not diminished with time.

O, reform it altogether; and let those that play your clowns speak no more than is set down for them; for there be of them that will themselves laugh to set on some quantity of barren spectators to laugh too, though in the mean time some necessary question of the play be then to be considered. That's villanous, and shows a most pitiful ambition in the fool that uses it.[5]

The advantages of touring under canvas have disappeared with changing times. In the first place, it is no longer necessary to bring theatre to small communities; the automobile allows audiences to drive distances of 100 miles and more to see productions in the larger cities. And now television can transport drama into the home, so that contemporary auditors need go no farther than their refrigerators. In addition, vacant lots located in midtown areas have disappeared; tent shows found it was a great disadvantage to set up in a field at the outskirts of a community where their presence was easily ignored. And, finally, managers can no longer attract show personnel. Union wages in industry have lured away both actors and canvasmen.

By following weekly accounts in *Billboard* that continued as late as the mid-1950's, until coin machines and phonograph recordings became the new trade emphasis, the story of the decline of tent shows can be clearly plotted. Hundreds of companies closed during the depression years, never to reopen. World War II, with its drain on personnel and its gas rationing, did away with many of the remaining tent troupes. Following the war, a vestige of a dozen or more shows carried on until one by one they disappeared. The single remaining company on the road today, the Schaffner Players, under the management of James and Juanita Davis, is a museum piece, representing what was once an energetic industry. The recent organizing of The National Society for the Preservation of Tent, Folk and Repertoire Theatre is a clear admission that the day of the tent show is over.

NOTES

Chapter I

[1]In Ohio, Shawnee township farmers built an opera house with money accumulated from taxes on Standard Oil property, which caused a writer for the *Dramatic Mirror* to observe, "This is undoubtedly the most unique playhouse, considering its environment and the circumstances of its erection, in the world. . . . Surely it cannot be more than a one-night stand theatre, and probably one attraction a month would be all that could find profit in it." New York *Dramatic Mirror*, June 29, 1907, p. 4. In Stephenson, Michigan, small town determination was shown when a Roman Catholic priest, disturbed because there was no opera house, converted the parish house into a theatre and began booking attractions. New York *Dramatic Mirror*, June 28, 1902, p. 2.

[2]Arthur Hornblow, *A History of the Theatre in America* (2 Vols.; New York, Benjamin Blom, Inc., 1965), I, 172-73.

[3]*Ibid.*, p. 25.

[4]New York *Dramatic Mirror*, January 6, 1906, p. 11.

[5]Some opera houses were built by wealthy citizens as a gesture of civic appreciation and for the honor of placing the family name on the cornice. One such person was Ambrose A. Call. The Call Opera House in Algona, Iowa, completed in 1892, was operated by the Call family for many years. Lewis Atherton, *Main Street on the Middle Border* (Bloomington, University of Indiana Press, 1954), p. 137.

[6]Willis Frederick Dunbar, "The Opera House as a Social Institution in Michigan," *Michigan History Magazine*, XXVII (October-December, 1943), p. 668.

[7]*Billboard*, April 23, 1949, pp. 54, 108.

[8]New York *Dramatic Mirror*, September 5, 1896, p. 2.

[9]The show carried a rube band as an attraction, a common feature with small companies playing to a rural patronage. Clipping from *Billboard*, n.d. Charles L. Davis used a band with the *Alvin Joslin* company as early as 1879. Later, Davis toured two bands with the *A Social Session* company, one uniformed and one in rural attire; both bands participated in a noon parade, end-

ing at a main public square for a concert. *Ibid.*

[10]William H. Crane, "The Modern Cart of Thespis," *North American Review*, CLIV (April, 1892), p. 474.

[11]*Ibid.*, p. 475.

[12]New York *Dramatic Mirror*, June 25, 1892, p. 4.

[13]New York *Dramatic Mirror*, July 2, 1892, p. 4.

[14]New York *Dramatic Mirror*, May 10, 1902, p. 14.

[15]Alfred L. Bernheim, *The Business of the Theatre* (New York, Benjamin Blom, Inc., 1964), p. 34.

Chapter II

[1]Alwin Thaler, "Strolling Players and Provincial Drama After Shakespeare," *PMLA*, XXXVII (June, 1922), p. 244.

[2]Clayton Hamilton, "Melodrama, Old and New," *Bookman*, XXXIII (May, 1911), p. 312.

[3]Felix Reichmann, "Amusements in Lancaster, 1750-1940," *Lancaster County Historical Society*, XLV (1941), p. 49.

[4]*Billboard*, March 9, 1918, p. 22.

[5]At one time Corse Payton, a successful actor-manager, maintained a scenic studio in Brocton, Massachusetts, where two artists prepared "new special mountings." New York *Dramatic Mirror*, June 2, 1897, p. 3. Another manager, Charles K. Champlin, kept artists working throughout the summer lay-off. One particular set, designed by Champlin himself, was "decorated and ornamented with cut glass in imitation of diamonds and rubies." New York *Dramatic Mirror*, April 11, 1903, p. 2. James Waite's New Stock Company advertised in 1898: "Every set of each play staged with special and beautiful scenery, calcium and other effects." *Billboard*, April 2, 1898, (advertisement), p. 11.

[6]Charles R. Phipps, letter to Fannie Henderson, January 11, 1949. Michigan actor Bert C. Arnold, in claiming that companies respected each others' territory, explained it as understandable since "most were using the same plays." He remembers the popular attractions included *East Lynne, St. Elmo, Camille, Way Down East, Trail of the Lonesome Pine, Ten Nights in a Bar Room, Uncle Tom's Cabin, The Hidden Hand, Grit the Newsboy, Shepherd of the Hills,* and *Lena Rivers.* Bert C. Arnold, letter to William Slout, March 30, 1965.

[7]*Billboard*, January 26, 1907, p. 4.

[8]George W. Stevens, Sr. (Dr. Judd), "The Old Wagon Days with Theatrical Companies," New York *Dramatic Mirror*, Dec. 20, 1902, p. x.

[9]A member of the troupe was Miss Ada B. Menken who, according to the press, "is yet quite young, and has a bright future before her." Oran Teague, *Professional Theatre in Louisianna* (Unpublished M. A. Thesis, Louisianna: Louisianna State University, 1952), pp. 13-20.

[10]Donald J. Rulfs, "The Professional Theatre in Wilmington, 1870-1900," *North Carolina Historical Review*, XXXVIII (October, 1951), p. 318.

11Oran Teague, *Professional Theatre in Louisiana.*

12Henriette Naeseth, "Drama in Early Deadwood, 1876-1879," *American Literature*, X (November, 1938), pp. 292-93. Other organizations of the 1870's were headed by such names as Jake Simon, Felix and Eva Vincent, the Wallace Sisters, J. W. Carner, John F. Breyer, George Walters, George Maxwell, Charles Forbes, H. A. Kendall, Jack Turner, Horace Herbert, and Jack Hogan. *Billboard*, March 2, 1918, pp. 20, 22.

13Marian Spitzer, "Ten-Twenty-Thirty, the Passing of the Popular-Priced Circuit," *Saturday Evening Post*, CXCVIII (August 22, 1925), p. 42. Payton knew what appealed to his audiences; his performances were enhanced by colorful sets and costumes. Etta Reed, his wife and leading lady, was said to have appeared in as many as fifty-two different gowns each week. New York *Dramatic Mirror*, February 13, 1897, p. 2.

14New York *Dramatic Mirror*, May 22, 1897, p. 13.

15*Ibid.*

16M. F. Ketchum, *Born to Be an Actor* (Published by the author, Newton Iowa, Ketchie Print Shop, n.d.), pp. 3-5.

17Luke Cosgrave, *Theatre Tonight* (Hollywood, House-Warven, 1952), p. 32.

18*Billboard*, August 28, 1948, p. 49.

19*Billboard*, November 30, 1940, p. 10.

Chapter III

1The Pennsylvania Railroad had recently sent out a notice that no more than ten pieces of scenery could be checked as baggage, which forced the smaller companies to put on a special baggage car when using the Pennsylvania line. *Billboard*, March 16, 1907, p. 41.

2New York *Dramatic Mirror*, April 24, 1897, p. 12.

3New York *Dramatic Mirror*, July 20, 1901, p. 12.

4*Harper's Weekly*, August 8, 1891, p. 595.

5A. R. Rogers, "Advice to Street Railway Managers of Parks," *Billboard*, March 23, 1901, p. 17.

6In writing of the stock companies days (circa 1875) at the Walnut Street Theatre in Philadelphia, Otis Skinner stated that manuscripts of privately owned plays did not contain the complete texts; speeches of supporting actors were written out in full, but the stars' lines were only represented by the cue words. Such playbooks were referred to at that time as "skeleton manuscripts." Otis Skinner, *Footlights and Spotlights*, (New York, Blue Ribbon Books, 1924), p. 57.

7New York *Dramatic Mirror*, Christmas Issue, 1898, p. 44. Burton and Sanger's Players was charged with changing the title of *Jane* to *A Wife Wanted*, *My Partner* to *Shadows of Shasta*, and *Our Wildcat* to *Struck Gas*. New York *Dramatic Mirror*, May 22, 1897, p. 2. The company of Harry Sheldon and Hazel Harrison was accused of presenting *The Plunge* under the title of *Dangers of a Great City*, *Pawn Ticket* as *Ten in Kentucky*, *In Old Kentucky* as *My Old Kentucky Home*, and *La Belle Marie* as *A Woman's Revenge*. *Ibid.*

8New York *Dramatic Mirror*, November 18, 1893, p. 3.

[9]New York *Dramatic Mirror*, May 25, 1895, p. 16.

[10]Such an operator was A. F. Helm of Lexington, Kentucky, who offered such copyrighted plays as *Hazel Kirke*, *Lynwood*, *M'liss*, *The Old Homestead*, *The White Slave*, and *Esmeralda* for from three to six dollars each. At this same time the Southern Manuscript Company in Swainsboro, Georgia, was advertising "any play you want for $300;" and W. Gault Browne was sending out circulars from a small Illinois town, offering copyrighted plays for three dollars each or two for five dollars. New York *Dramatic Mirror*, June 27, 1896, p. 9; July 11, 1896, p. 9; October 31, 1896, p. 13.

[11]New York *Dramatic Mirror*, November 4, 1893, p. 3.

[12]New York *Dramatic Mirror*, March 16, 1895, p. 8.

[13]New York *Dramatic Mirror*, February 13, 1892, p. 8; December 1, 1894, p. 11.

[14]New York *Dramatic Mirror*, July 11, 1896, p. 9.

[15]New York *Dramatic Mirror*, January 16, 1897, pp. 11-14.

[16]New York *Dramatic Mirror*, November 5, 1898, p. 23.

[17]"A Theatre with a 5,000,000 Audience," *World's Work*, XX (May, 1910), p. 12876.

[18]New York *Dramatic Mirror*, June 22, 1907, p. 14.

Chapter IV

[1]Lily B. Campbell, *Scenes and Machines on the English Stage During the Renaissance* (New York, Barnes and Noble, Inc., 1960), pp. 123-24.

[2]George C. D. Odell, *Annals of the New York Stage* (New York, Columbia University Press, 1927-1949), III, p. 75. Barriere was the proprietor of an ice cream parlor on Chatham Street, which earned him a modest prosperity. He erected a "small temporary stage under a canvas roof" for concerts and musical dramas, and operated in this manner for a number of years, until he was "compelled to build a fireproof edifice, or abandon his flimsy canvas theatre." Charles Durang, "The Philadelphia Stage from the Year 1794 to the Year 1855," Philadelphia *Sunday Dispatch*, 1854-1860, Chapter XXI, p. 211.

[3]"An Automobile Theatre," *Theatre*, XI (May, 1911), p. 169.

[4]An example of this occurred in 1916 when the Williams Stock Company was playing in Hendersonville, North Carolina. Ten sections of "blues" went down, injuring a number of people. No suits were brought against the company; but all liabilities were settled by the management. *Billboard*, September 16, 1916, p. 16.

Chapter V

[1]Fayette Lodawick Robinson, "Dilly Fay, the Clown: A Reminiscence of a Showman's Life," New York *Clipper*, February 17, 1872, p. 364. Included in Robinson's company were actors Charles Wilson and Theodore Luff. Athlic Smith was the orchestra leader; Ferdinand Hopp led the band. A. S. Burt was the advance agent.

[2]New York *Dramatic Mirror*, July 17, 1886, p. 1.

[3]*Billboard*, February 14, 1948, p. 78; February 28, 1948, p. 77. Others frequently identified with early tent repertoire are J. C. Rockwell and J. Al Sawtelle; both managers were touring in the East around 1893. *Billboard*, January 19, 1918, p. 22; March 30, 1918, p. 22.

[4]The following repertoire companies were operating under canvas prior to 1910. The list is by no means complete. Chase-Lister Stock Company, Harrison Stock Company, Kinsey Komedy Kompany, Bybee Standard Stock Company, William F. Lewis Stock Company, Sterling Dramatic Company, Minnelli Brothers, Viola Wilson Repertoire Company, Angell's Comedians, Copeland Brothers, Ginnivan Stock Company, Williams Stock Company, The Great Shortridge Shows, Elwin Strong Dramatic Company, Harry Shannon Stock Company, Norwood's Big Canvas Theatre, Irene Jeavons Stock Company, Mason and Imson's Pavilion Theatre, Hogate's Dramatic Company, Grandi Stock Company, Criterion Stock Company, George H. Pawlus' Empire Stock Company, Buckeye Stock company, Perce R. Benton's Comedians, Bennett's Big Dramatic Company, Austin and Cole's Dramatic Company, Crawford's Comedians, Bessie Curley Stock Company, Kelly Stock Company, Miller Stock Company, Peters' Peerless Company, W. I. Swain Dramatic Company, Maxam and Sights' Comedians, Roy E. Fox's Popular Players, Rosar's Comedians, Choate's Comedians Callahan Dramatic Company, Rentfrow's Jolly Pathfinders.

[5]J. C. Furnas, *Goodbye to Uncle Tom* (New York, William Sloane, 1956), p. 282.

[6]Bruce Bliven, "Mother, Home and Heaven," *The New Republic*, XXXVII, (January 9, 1924), p. 173.

[7]Harry P. Harrison, *Culture Under Canvas: The Story of Tent Chautauqua* (As told to Karl Detzer; New York, Hastings House, Publishers, 1958), p. 194.

[8]Victoria Case, *We Called It Culture* (Garden City, New York, Doubleday and Company, Inc., 1948), p. 54.

[9]*Ibid.*, p. 52.

[10]New York *Dramatic Mirror*, February 9, 1901, p. 14.

[11]New York *Dramatic Mirror*, January 20, 1906, p. 12.

[12]*Ibid.*, p. 14.

[13]Louis Verneuil, *The Fabulous Life of Sarah Bernhardt* (New York, Harper and Brothers, 1942), p. 256.

[14]New York *Dramatic Mirror*, January 20, 1906, p. 12.

[15]William F. Conner, "My Impressions of Sarah Bernhardt," *Theatre*, XV, (October, 1915), p. 173.

[16]New York *Dramatic Mirror*, April 7, 1906, p. 9.

[17]Ted North, taped interview, May 1, 1965.

[18]*Billboard*, April 28, 1906, p. 3.

[19]San Francisco *Chronicle*, July 1, 1906, p. 26.

[20]Edwin Emerson, Jr., "San Francisco at Play," *Sunset Magazine*, XVII (October, 1906), p. 326.

Chapter VI

[1]*Billboard*, December 27, 1919, p. 14.

[2]*Billboard*, February 14, 1920, p. 22. In 1918 both Choate's Comedians and the Amazon Brothers show reported the best business in over twenty years. The following year, tent showman John Lawrence stated that "during the past couple of years a 'bloomer' has been rare in occurrence with any of the better repertoire shows through the Middle West;" and the Hunt Stock Company boasted of having "one of the most prosperous years in the history of the show." *Billboard*, October 5, 1918, p. 19; November 16, 1918, p. 19; March 22, 1919, p. 33; August 20, 1919, p. 29.

[3]Mark Sullivan, *Our Times* (New York, Scribner's, 1933) V, pp. 377-378.

[4]Luke Cosgrave, *Theatre Tonight* (Hollywood, House-Warven, 1952), p. 188.

[5]Bert J. Chipman, *Hey Rube* (Hollywood, Hollywood Print Shop, 1933), pp. 79-80.

[6]Ted North, taped interview, May 1, 1965.

[7]*Billboard*, January 27, 1917, p. 16. The William F. Lewis Stock Company loaded its show wagons on flat cars and moved them circus-style from place to place. *Billboard*, April 8, 1916, p. 16.

[8]*Billboard*, May 22, 1920, p. 14.

[9]*Billboard*, August 30, 1919, p. 29. Two years earlier, when Hicker found he would be unable to make a scheduled opening on time, a special train was chartered in Toledo to take the company the twenty-seven miles to Delta (Ohio). *Billboard*, July 28, 1917, p. 24.

[10]Floyd Clymer, *Floyd Clymer's Historical Motor Scrapbook* (Los Angeles, Clymer Motors, 1944), pp. 75, 76, 96.

[11]"How the Circus Dodges the Railroad Blockade," *Literary Digest*, LVI (March 16, 1918), pp. 87-88.

[12]*Billboard*, July 6, 1918, p. 17.

[13]John D. Hicks, *Republican Ascendancy* (New York, Harper & Row, 1963), p. 19.

[14]Tent repertoire companies operating between 1914-20 included Allmann Comedy Co., Amazon Brothers, American Stock Co., Attebery Dramatic Co., Aulger Brothers, Angell's Comedians, Baird and Wilson, Belle Barchus Players, Baughman-Gustine, Benner Repertoire Co., Bettis Comedians, Beveridge Repertoire Co., Blair's Comedians, Blondin Repertoire Co., Brownie Blye Stock Co., Bowers Overland Show Co., Brady Players, Brennan Dramatic Co., Brown and Brenner, Brunk's Comedians, Boyd Burrows Repertoire Tent Co., Bybee Standard Stock Co., Callahan Dramatic Co., Carroll Comedy Co., Carter Dramatic Co., Chase-Lister Stock Co., Choate's Comedians, Clark's Comedians, Clifton Comedy Co., Colonial Stock Co., Compton-Plumb Stock Co., Conger and Santo, Copeland Brothers Stock Co., Crawford's Comedians, Crawley's Comedians, Curtis-McDonald's Comedians, Dalley Stock Co., Lawrence Deming Theatre Co., Demorest Stock Co., Flora DeVoss Repertoire Co., Dubinsky Brothers, Edwards-Wilson Repertoire Co., Engesser's Dramatic Tent Show, Engle Brothers Overland Show, Paul English Stock Co., The John G. and Little

Fern Co., Florence Players, Fontinelle Stock Co., Roy E. Fox's Popular Players, That Franklin Show, Gagnon-Pollock Stock Co., Gerrard Stock Co., Frank Ginnivan Stock Co., Norma Ginnivan Stock Co., Gordinier Grothers, Al Gorrell Repertoire Co., Grenwood Amusement Co., Guy Players, Sewell's Halcyon Players, Ollie Hamilton Repertoire Co., Charles Harrison Stock Co., Haswell Stock Co., Earl Hawk Big Stock Co., Marie Hayes and Her Excellent Players, James Heffner-Ina Lehr Stock Co., Herbert-Gilpin Stock Co., Hillman Stock Co., Hugo Players, Hunt Stock Co., Ingram Players, Jennings Tent Theatre Co., Justus-Romaine, Keene Komedy Kompany, Lanshawe Players, LaRoy Stock Co., LaViolette Players, John Lawrence Stock Co., William F. Lewis Stock Co., Lester Lindsey Stock Co., Guy E. Long's Associated Players, Lowery Brothers, Mac Stock Co., Maddock's Park Players, Manville Brothers, Marshall Players, Melville's Comedians, Miller Brothers, Minnelli Brothers, Hila Morgan Stock Co., J. Doug Morgan Stock Co., Murphy's Comedians, Mac-Taff Co., Nash-Townley Repertoire Co., Nevision Players, Ralph E. Nicol's Comedians, North Brothers Stock Co., Ed. C. Nutt Comedy Players, Paling Players, Paramount Players, Paul Brothers-Wolford Stock Co., Pitman Stock Co., Plumlee's Comedians, Pommier Tent Theatre Co., Price-Butler, Princess Stock Co., Pullin's Comedians, John G. Rae Dramatic Co., Dorothy Reeves Stock Co., Reliable Brandon Show, Rentfrow's Jolly Pathfinders, Ripley's Big Tent Show, Ripple and Lee, George Roberson Players, Helen B. Ross Co., Dr. H. D. Rucker's Repertoire Co., Walter Savidge Players, Harry Shannon Stock Co., Edna Spangler Co., Byron Spaun Show, Charlie Starr's Liberty Players, Starnes Stock Co., Steele and Whittington's Comedians, Elwin Strong Dramatic Co., Swafford Players, W. I. Swain Dramatic Co., Swan's Dramatic Show, George Sweet Players, Toby Players, Tolbert Big Tent Theatre, Herbert Walters Players, Warner Stock Co., Ben Wilkes Big Tent Shows, L. B. Wesselman Stock Co., West-DeForest Players, Whitney Stock Co., Barney Williams Players, Wolverton Stock Co.,Woodward and West, Wood-Ray Stock Co., Charles Wortham Dramatic Co.,

The above is not a complete listing.

Chapter VII

[1]New York *Dramatic Mirror*, January 14, 1899, p. 18.
[2]New York *Dramatic Mirror*, April 1, 1899, p. 15.
[3]*Ibid.*
[4]Rose's sister, Ida, toured in a rural comedy called *Sis Hopkins' Sister.* New York *Dramatic Mirror*, May 7, 1904, p. 15. Rose Melville did not originate the Sis Hopkins name. A play copyrighted in 1877, *Sis Hopkins, the Country Girl,* was written by Charles H. Boyle and Carrie Graham. *Dramatic Compositions copyrighted in the United States,* II. It is possible that she performed in this piece during her early days in western repertoire.
[5]Richard M. Dorson, "The Yankee on the Stage—a Folk Hero of American Drama," *New England Quarterly*, XIII (September, 1940), p. 490. As Dorson suggests, Rip Van Winkle was the beginning of a popular taste for eccentric old men that led to such modern examples as Lightnin' Bill Jones, Jeeter Lester, and the two grandpas in *On Borrowed Time* and *You Can't Take It With You.*

[6]Arthur Hobson Quinn, *Drama from the Civil War to the Present Day* (New York, Appleton-Century-Crofts, 1964), p. 128.

[7]*Billboard*, January 3, 1925, p. 28.

[8]Mary North, taped interview.

[9]Typewritten copy of *Saintly Hypocrites and Honest Sinners* in the collection of this writer.

[10]Mimeographed copy of *The Only Road* in the collection of this writer.

[11]An explanation of Wilson and his connection with the origin of Toby will be included in the next chapter.

[12]Typewritten copy of *The Awakening of John Slater* in the collection of this writer. Harrison's first copyrighted play, *Clover Dale*, was registered in 1904. This was followed by *Her Cowboy Visitor* and *The Signal Fire* (1905); *The Love of a Thief, In the Days of Auld Lang Syne*, and *Doctor's Prescription* (1906); *Just June, The Lone Star Ranch*, and *Mr. John Graham of New York* (1911); *Winona* (1912); *The Nest of Crime, A Prince of the Range*, and *The Turn of a Card* (1915).

[13]New York *Dramatic Mirror*, March 13, 1909, pp. 2, 7.

[14]Typed copy of *Call of the Woods* in the collection of this writer, p. 6.

[15]*Call of the Woods*, p. 28.

[16]*Ibid*.p. 33.

[17]Charles F. Horner, *Strike the Tents, the Story of the Chautauqua* (Dorrance and Company, 1954), p. 183.

[18]Joseph E. Gould, *The Chautauqua Movement* (State University of New York, 1961), p. 83.

[19]Richard Hofstadter, *The Age of Reform* (New York, Alfred A. Knopf. Inc., 1955), p. 24.

[20]*Ibid.*, p. 27.

[21]*Ibid.*, p. 30.

[22]Norman Holland, "The Country Wife," *The First Modern Comedies* (Bloomington, Indiana University Press, 1959), Chapter VIII.

[23]Hofstadter, *The Age of Reform*, p. 34.

[24]William E. Leuchtenburg, *The Perils of Prosperity, 1914-32* (Chicago, University of Chicago Press, 1958), p. 168.

[25]Zelda F. Popkin, "The Tent Show Turns to Sex," *Outlook and Independent*, CLVI (September 24, 1930), p. 30.

Chapter VIII

[1]Allardyce Nicoll, *Masks, Mimes and Miracles* (New York, Cooper Square Publishers, Inc., 1963), p. 43.

[2]Boris Ford, (ed.), *The Age of Shakespeare* (Baltimore, Penguin Books, 1955), p. 34.

[3]Later examples can be seen in Sheridan's Tony Lumpkin, Shadwell's Sir Timothy Shacklehead, and Steele's Humphry Gubbin.

[4]William Dunlap, *History of the American Theatre, and Anecdotes of the Principal Actors* (New York, Burt Franklin, 1963) p. 156.

[5]Odell, *Annals of the American Stage*, I, pp. 239, 242.

[6]Dunlap, *History of the American Theatre*, p. 153.

[7]*Ibid.*, p. 119.

[8]Dunlap, *History of the American Theatre*, p. 160.

[9]*Ibid.*

[10]William Dunlap, "Darby's Return," *America's Lost Plays*, XXI, Walter J. Meserve and William R. Reardon, eds. (Bloomington, Indiana, Indiana University Press, 1969), p. 111.

[11]See reprint included here.

[12]See reprint included here.

[13]Royall Tyler, "The Contrast," *Dramas for the American Theatre*, Richard Moody, ed. (Cleveland, World Publishing Company, 1966), p. 58. Wignell also performed Darby in O'Keeffe's *Love in a Camp, or Patrick in Prussia*, a sequel to *The Poor Soldier*, first produced in New York in 1787. The play, originally done at Covent Garden two years earlier, never received the popularity in England or America as the former piece.

[14]In *Darby's Return*, Darby makes reference to his hair of "carrot-colour." William Dunlap, "Darby's Return," *America's Lost Plays*, XXI, p. 109.

[15]Anna Cora Mowatt has described the representative Yankee character as having a "red wig, striped pantaloons that maintained a respectable distance from his ankles, a short jacket, and a flame-colored cravat." *Autobiography of an Actress* (Boston, Ticknor, Reed, and Field, 1854), p. 259. In the 19th century, William Poel wore a red wig and baggy clothes in a serio-comic portrayal of Shylock; and in *Hobbies*, Nat Goodwin's Professor Pygmalion Whiffles was performed in a bald pate fringed with red.

[16]A farce, amplifying the Christopher Sly character in *Taming of the Shrew*, was written by Christopher Bullocks and performed in 1715 under the title *The Cobler of Preston*. The Sly facsimile was Toby Guzzle, an inebriated rustic. Early 19th century models include Toby Thatch in *The London Hermit, or Rambles in Dorsetshire*, written in 1793 by John O'Keeffe; Frederick Reynolds' farce *Arbitration, or Free and Easy*, which has in its cast a Sir Toby Tritely; Toby Heywood in *The Rent Day* by Douglas Jerrold; and a farce by W. B. Bernard, *The Mummy*, with a Toby Tramp. A more modern example is Charles A. Krone's "quaint and homely" character, Squire Tobias, in *The Country Squire*, first produced in 1893. The play was a domestic drama which drew its inspiration from American country life.

[17]*The British Theatre; or a Collection of Plays, Which were Acted at Drury Lane, Covent Garden, and Haymarket*, biographical and critical remarks by Mrs. Inchbald (London, Longman, Hurst, Rees, and Orme, 1808), XXV, p. 3.

[18]Thomas Morton and J. M. Morton, *All That Glitters Is Not Gold* (New York, Harold Roorbach, 1889), p. 13.

[19]Odell, *Annals of the American Stage*, VI, pp. 11, 43, 52; VII, p. 35; VIII, p. 500; X, p. 36.

[20]*Dramatic Compositions*, I, p. 1565; II, p. 2641. The play is also called *Tobe Hoxie*.

[21]Ernest Lamson, *Tobe Hoxie.* Manuscript in the University of Chicago Library.

[22]Review and display advertisement from a Milwaukee paper in the theatre collection of the New York Public Library, (n.d.).

[23]Robert Downing, "Toby," *Theatre Arts* (November, 1946), pp. 651-54.

[24]Since Downing's article appeared in 1946, a host of magazine and newspaper stories have been issued as well as a dissertation at the University of Illinois by Larry Dale Clark (Clark, "Toby Shows: a Form of American Popular Theatre," 1963); another at the University of Minnesota by Sherwood Snyder, III, (Snyder, "The Toby Shows," 1966); as well as a scholarly essay by Dr. Jere C. Mickell for the *Journal of American Folklore* (Mickel, "The Genesis of Toby," *Journal of American Folklore*, LXXX, October-November, 1967, pp. 334-40). And, finally, a book has been recently published, reminiscences of the most famous modern day Toby, Neil Schaffner, which includes suggestions about Toby's origin (Neil Schaffner and Vance Johnson, *The Fabulous Toby and Me,* Englewood Cliffs, N. J., Prentice-Hall, Inc., 1968).

[25]Downing, "Toby," p. 653.

[26]Clark, "Tent Shows: a Form of American Popular Theatre," p. 99.

[27]Snyder uses the correct spelling of the Louisiana town.

[28]Snyder, "The Toby Shows," pp. 15-16.

[29]Mickel, "The Genesis of Toby," pp. 335-36.

[30]*Ibid.,* p. 337.   [31]Schaffner and Johnson, *The Fabulous Toby and Me,* p. 5.
[32]*Ibid.*

[33]Mickel, "The Genesis of Toby," p. 336; Robert L Sherman, *Drama Cyclopedia* (Chicago, Published by the Author, 1944).

[34]Horace Murphy, taped interview, September 20, 1967.

[35]American Theatre program for week commencing March 14, 1904; New York *Dramatic Mirror,* March 19, 1904, p. 16; New York *Herald,* March 9, 1904.

[36]New York *Dramatic Mirror,* April 9, 1904, p. 7; April 16, 1904, p. 8; April 23, 1904, p. 10; April 30, 1904, p. 8; May 7, 1904, p. 9; May 14, 1904, p. 8.

[37]Chicago *Daily Tribune,* June 22, 1903.

[38]Chicago *Sentinel,* August 25, 1904.

[39]Chicago *News,* October 10, 1905.

[40]Program of Castle Square Theatre for week commencing April 13, 1908.

[41]Nashville *American,* November 15, 1904.

[42]Clipping, Milwaukee, Wisconsin, April 8, 1909.

[43]Murphy, taped interview September 20, 1967.

[44]*Billboard,* June 24, 1911, p. 17.

[45]*Billboard,* December 18, 1920, p. 37.

[46]Murphy, taped interviews September 20, 25, 1967.

[47]Murphy, taped interview September 20, 1967

[48]Murphy, taped interview September 25, 1967.

[49]Murphy, taped interview September 20, 1967.   [50]*Ibid.*

[51]Letter from Byron E. Walton to Neil Schaffner September 2, 1962.

[52]*Dramatic Compositions Copyrighted in the United States*, I, p. 363.

[53]Clippings from New York *Telegraph,* March 8, 1904; Chicago *Daily Tribune,* June 22, 1902; New York *Times,* March 8, 1904; New York *Herald,* March 9, 1904; Nashville *Daily News,* November 15, 1904; Nashville *American,* November 15, 1904; Nashville *Banner,* November 15, 1904; New York *Dramatic Mirror,* March 19, 1904, p. 16.

Chapter IX

[1]Charles Wortham stored in tiny Blue Mound, Illinois; Bennett's Big Show in Milaca, Minnesota; Carter Dramatic Company in Marne, Michigan; Choate's Comedians in Cambria, Illinois; and the Ginnivan Stock Company in Fayette, Ohio. On the other hand, W. I. Swain, who had several shows on the road, boasted of an entire city block in New Orleans.

[2]Frank Emmett, "Trouping Under Canvas," *Billboard,* December 9, 1911, pp. 24, 94.

[3]Cleveland Moffett, "How the Circus is Put Up and Taken Down," *McClure's Magazine,* V (June, 1895), p. 49.

[4]Guy Forrest, taped interview, September 2, 1967.

[5]Ermin Gray, taped interview, September 2, 1967.

[6]Neil Schaffner, taped interview, September 2, 1967.

[7]*Billboard,* January 26, 1924, p. 28.

[8]The first band Murphy led for his own company included Merle Evans, who later became the reknowned bandmaster for Ringling Brothers Circus. Murphy, taped interview, September 25, 1967.

[9]Mason Wilkes, taped interview, September 1, 1967.

[10]*Billboard,* May 19, 1906, p. 26.

[11]R. W. G. Vail, *Random Notes on The History of the Early American Circus* (Worcester, Massachusetts, American Antiquarian Society, 1934), p. 91.

[12]*Billboard,* March 18, 1916, p. 44.

Commentary

[1]J. C. Furnas, *Goodbye to Uncle Tom* (New York, William Sloane Associates, 1956), p. 281.

[2]Harry L. Dixon, "Doff Your Hat to the Tent Show," *Billboard,* March 20, 1926, p. 13.

[3]Alfred Bernheim, *The Business of the Theatre* (New York, Benjamin Blom, Inc., 1964), p. 99.

[4]Skinner, *Footlights and Spotlights*, p. 41.

[5]*Hamlet* III.ii.42-50.

BIBLIOGRAPHY

A. BOOKS

Allen, Frederick Lewis, *The Big Change, 1900-1950*. New York, Harper & Row, 1952.

Anderson, John, *The American Theatre*. New York, Dial Press, 1938.

Atherton, Lewis, *Main Street on the Middle Border*. Bloomington, University of Indiana Press, 1954.

Barnum, P. T., *Barnum's Own Story*. New York, Dover Publications, Inc., 1961.

————, *Struggles and Triumphs: or Forty Years' Recollections*. Hartford, J. B. Burr & Company, 1870.

Beer, Thomas, *The Mauve Decade*. New York, Vintage Books, 1960.

Bernhardt, Lysiane, *Sarah Bernhardt, My Grandmother*. Trans. Vyvyan Holland. London, Hurst and Blackett Ltd., 1949.

Bernheim, Alfred, *The Business of the Theatre*. New York, Benjamin Blom, Inc., 1964.

Bieber, Margarete, *The History of the Greek and Roman Theatre*. London, Oxford University Press, 1961.

Birdoff, Harry, *The World's Greatest Hit—Uncle Tom's Cabin*. New York, S. F. Vanni, 1947.

Blum, Daniel, *A Pictorial History of the American Theatre*. New York, Greenberg Publisher, 1950.

Brown, T. Allston, *History of the American Stage*. 1870.

_____, *A History of the New York Stage from the First Performance in 1732 to 1901*. 3 vols. New York, Dodd, Mead and Company, 1903.

Campbell, Lilly B., *Scenes and Machines on the English Stage During the Renaissance*. New York, Barnes and Noble, Inc., 1960.

Case, Victoria and Robert Ormond Case, *We Called It Culture*. Garden City, N. Y., Doubleday and Company, Inc., 1948.

Chindahl, George L., *A History of the Circus in America*. Caldwell, Idaho, Caxton Printers, 1959.

Chipman, Bert J., *Hey Rube*. Hollywood, Hollywood Print Shop, 1933.

Clymer, Floyd, *Floyd Clymer's Historical Motor Scrapbook*. Los Angeles, Clymer Motors, 1944.

Commager, Henry Steele, *The American Mind*. New Haven, Yale University Press, 1950.

Cosgrave, Luke, *Theatre Tonight*. Hollywood, House-Warven, 1952.

Crawford, Mary Caroline, *Romance of the American Theatre*. Boston, Little, Brown, 1927.

Crosse, Gordon, *Shakespearean Playgoing, 1890-1952*. London, A. R. Mowbray and Co., 1953.

Dimmick, Ruth C., *Our Theatres Today and Yesterday*. New York, 1913.

Doherty, Edward, *The Rain Girl, the Tragic Story of Jeanne Eagels*. Philadelphia, Macrae, Smith & Co., 1930.

Dulles, Foster Rhea, *America Learns to Play*. Gloucester, Massachusetts, Peter Smith, 1940.

Dunlap, William, *History of the American Theatre, and Anecdotes of the Principal Actors*. New York, Burt Franklin, 1963.

Durant, John and Alice Durant, *Pictorial History of the American Circus*. New York, A. S. Barnes and Co., 1957.

Ernst, Alice Henson, *Trouping in the Oregon Country: A History of Frontier Theatre*. Portland, Oregon, Oregon Historical Society, 1961.

Faulkner, Harold U., *Politics, Reform and Expansion: 1890-1900*. New York, Harper & Row, 1959.

Fellows, Dexter and Andrew A. Freeman, *This Way to the Big Show*. New York, Halcyon House, 1938.

Ford, Boris (ed.), *The Age of Shakespeare*. Baltimore, Penguin Books, 1955.

Fox, Charles Philip, *Circus Parades, A Pictorial History of America's Greatest Pageant*. Watkins Glen, New York, Century House, 1953.

_____, *Ticket to the Circus*. New York, Bramhall House, 1959.

Furnas, J. C., *Goodbye to Uncle Tom*. New York, William Sloane Associates, 1956.

Fyles, Franklin, *The Theatre and Its People*. New York, Doubleday, Page and Company, 1900.

Gilbert, Doublas, *American Vaudeville, Its Life and Times*. New York, Whittlesey House, 1940.

Goldman, Eric F., *Rendezvous with Destiny*. New York, Alfred A. Knopf, Inc., 1952.

Gould Joseph E., *The Chautauqua Movement*. New York, State University of New York, 1961.

Graham, Philip, *Showboats: The History of an American Institution.* Austin, University of Texas Press, 1951.

Gras, Norman Scott Brien, *A History of Agriculture in Europe and America.* New York, Crofts, 1946.

Greenwood, Isaac J., *The Circus, Its Origin and Growth Prior to 1835.* Publications of the Dunlap Society New Series, No. 5. New York, The Society, 1898.

Harrison, Harry P., *Culture Under Canvas: The Story of Tent Chautauqua.* As told to Karl Detzer. New York, Hastings House, Publishers, 1958.

Hicks, John D., *Republican Ascendancy.* New York, Harper & Row, 1965.

Hodge, Francis Richard, *Yankee Theatre: The Image of America on the Stage, 1825-1850.* Austin, University of Texas Press, 1965.

Hofstadter, Richard, *The Age of Reform.* New York, Alfred A. Knopf, Inc., 1955.

Holland, Norman, *The First Modern Comedies.* Bloomington, Indiana University Press, 1959.

Hornblow, Arthur, *A History of the Theatre in America.* Vol. I & II. New York, Benjamin Blom, Inc., 1956.

Horner, Charles F., *Strike the Tents, the Story of the Chautauqua.* Philadelphia, Dorrance & Company, 1954.

Hoyt, Harlow R., *Town Hall Tonight.* New York, Bramhall House, 1955.

Hughes, Leo, *A Century of English Farce.* Princeton, New Jersey, Princeton University Press, 1956.

Hultgren, Thor, *American Transportation in Prosperity and Depression.* Baltimore, Waverly Press, Inc., 1948.

Hungerford, Edward, *The Story of the Baltimore & Ohio Railroad.* New York, G. P. Putnam's Sons, 1928.

Jennings, John J., *Theatrical and Circus Life; or Secrets of the Stage, Green-Room and Sawdust Arena.* Chicago, Globe Publishing Co., 1886.

Jensen, Oliver (ed.), *The Nineties.* New York, American Heritage Publishing Co., 1967.

Ketchum, M. F., *Born to Be an Actor.* Published by the author. Newton, Iowa, Ketchie Print Shop. (n.d.)

Krows, Arthur Edwin, *Play Production in America.* New York, Henry Holt and Co., 1916.

Kusell, Maurice L. and M. S. Merritt, *Marquee Ballyhoo.* Los Angeles, Overland-Out West Publications, 1932.

Leuchtenburg, William E., *The Perils of Prosperity, 1914-32.* Chicago, University of Chicago Press, 1958.

Link, Arthur S., *American Epoch.* New York, Alfred A. Knopf, 1963.

──────, *Wilson, the New Freedom.* Princeton, New Jersey, Princeton University Press, 1956.

Logan, Olive, *Before the Footlights and Behind the Scenes.* Philadelphia, Parmelee and Co., 1870.

Lord, Walter, *The Good Years.* New York, Harper & Row, 1960.

MacLaren, Gay, *Morally We Roll Along.* Little Brown & Co., 1938.

May, Earl Chapin, *The Circus from Rome to Ringling*. New York, Duffield Books, 1964

May, Henry F., *The End of American Innocence*. Chicago, Quadrangle Books, 1964.

McKechnie, Samuel, *Popular Entertainments Through the Ages*. New York, Benjamin Blom, Inc., 1969.

McKennon, Marian, *Tent Show*. New York, Exposition Press, 1964.

McMillen, Wheeler, *Land of Plenty: The American Farm Story*. New York, Holt, Rinehart and Winston, 1961.

Meade, Edwards, *Doubling Back, the Autobiography of an Actor*. Chicago, Hammond Press, 1916.

Minnigerode, Meade, *The Fabulous Forties*. New York, G. P. Putnam's Sons, 1924.

Morris, Lloyd, *Postscript to Yesterday, American Life and Thought, 1896-1946*. New York, Harper & Row, 1965.

Moses, Montrose J., *The American Dramatist*. New York, Benjamin Blom, Inc., 1964.

Mowatt, Anna Corra, *Autobiography of an Actress*. Boston, Ticknor, Reed, and Field. 1854.

Mowry, George E., *The Era of Theodore Roosevelt and the Birth of Modern America, 1900-1912*. New York, Harper & Row, 1962.

Nicoll, Allardyce, *Masks, Mimes and Miracles*. New York, Cooper Square Publishers, Inc., 1963.

Overton, Richard C., *Burlington Route*. New York, Alfred A. Knopf, 1965.

Pitou, Augustus, *Masters of the Show*. New York, The Neale Publishing Co., 1914.

Poggi, Jack, *Theatre in America, the Impact of Economic Forces, 1870-1967*. Ithaca, New York, Cornell University Press, 1968.

Quinn, Arthur Hobson, *A History of the American Drama from the Beginning to the Civil War*. New York, Appleton-Century-Crofts, 1943.

_____, *A History of the American Drama from the Civil War to the Present Day*. New York, Appleton-Century-Crofts, 1964.

Rice, Edwin Leroy, *Monarchs of Minstrelsy*. New York, Kenny, 1911.

Richardson, Jeanna, *Sarah Bernhardt*. London, Max Reinhardt Ltd., 1956.

Robeson, David, *Al G. Barnes, Master Showman*. Caldwell, Idaho, Caxton Printers, 1936.

Rourke, Constance, *American Humor, a Study of the National Character*. Garden City, New York, Doubleday Anchor Books, 1953.

Rueff, Suze, *I Knew Sarah Bernhardt*. London, Frederick Muller, Ltd., 1951.

Schaffner, Neil E. and Vance Johnson, *The Fabulous Toby and Me*. Englewood Cliffs, New Jersey, Prentice-Hall, 1968.

Scott, Marian, *Chautauqua Caravan*. New York, Appleton-Century-Co., 1939.

Shannon, Fred A., *The Farmer's Last Frontier: Agriculture, 1860-1897*. New York, Harper & Row, 1968.

Sharpe, Ernest Jack, *One Life*. Grand Rapids, Michigan, The Dean-Hicks Co., 1950.

Sherman, Robert L., *Actors and Authors*. Chicago, the Author, 1951.

_____, *Drama Cyclopedia*. Chicago, the Author, 1944.

Skinner, Cornelia Otis *Madame Sarah.* New York, Dell Publishing Co., 1968.
Skinner, Otis, *Footlights and Spotlights.* New York, Blue Ribbon Books, 1924.
Smith, Henry Nash, *Virgin Land.* New York, Vintage Books, 1950.
Sobel, Bernard, *A Pictorial History of Vaudeville.* New York, Citadel Press, 1961.
Stover, John F., *American Railroads.* Chicago, University of Chicago Press, 1961.
Sullivan, Mark, *Our Times.* Vol. III. New York, Charles Scribner's Sons, 1930.
_____, *Our Times.* Vol. V. New York, Charles Scribner's Sons, 1933.
Vail, R. W. G., *Random Notes on the History of the Early American Circus.*
    Worcester, Massachusetts, American Antiquarian Society, 1934.
Verneuil, Louis, *The Fabulous Life of Sarah Bernhardt.* Trans. Ernest Boyd.
    New York, Harper & Brothers, 1942.
Walters, Herb, *Fifty Years Under Canvas.* Hugo, Oklahoma, Achme Publishing
    Co., 1962.
Warde, Frederick, *Fifty Years of Make-Believe.* New York, The International
    Press Syndicate, 1920.
Waugh, Frank A., *Outdoor Theatres.* Boston, Richard G. Badger, 1917.
Werner, M. R., *Barnum.* New York, Harcourt, Brace and Company, 1923.
Wittke, Carl, *Tambo and Bones.* Durham, Duke University Press, 1930.
Wright, Richardson, *Hawkers and Walkers in Early America.* Philadelphia, J. B.
    Lippincott Company, 1927.

B. LETTERS

Arnold, Bert C. Letter to William Slout, March 30, 1965.
Green, Merritt. Letter to William Slout, May 4, 1965.
Murphy, Horace. Letter to Neil Schaffner, May 15, 1964.
_____. Letter to Jere Mickel, April 8, 1965.
Phipps, Charles R. Letter to Fannie Henderson, January 11, 1949.
Walton, Byron E. Letter to Neil Schaffner, September 2, 1962.
Whitworth, Ruth. Letter to William Slout, May 12, 1965.

C. NEWSPAPERS

Big Rapids, *Pioneer*, August 21, 1951.
Billboard, numbers inclusive from 1900 to 1950.
Bill Bruno's Bulletin, December 16, 1937. Clipping.
Chicago *Daily Tribune*, June 22, 1903. Clipping.
Chicago *News*, October 10, 1905. Clipping.
Chicago *Sentinel*, August 25, 1904. Clipping.
Detroit *Free Press*, January 7, 1966, p. 4-B.
Lansing, *The State Journal*, November 29, 1936.
Nashville *American*, November 15, 1904. Clipping.
Nashville *Banner*, November 12, 1904. Clipping.
Nashville *Daily News*, November 15, 1904. Clipping.
New York *Dramatic Mirror*, numbers inclusive from 1886 to 1921.
New York *Herald*, March 9, 1904. Clipping.

New York *Journal*, March 8, 1904. Clipping.
New York *Sun*, March 8, 1904. Clipping.
New York *Telegraph*, March 8, 1904. Clipping.
New York *Times*, March 8, 1904. Clipping.
New York *World*, March 8, 1904. Clipping.
Ohio State Journal, February 24, 1881, p. 1.
San Francisco *Chronicle*, July 1, 1906, p. 26.

D. PERIODICALS

Albert, Allen D., "Tents of the Conservative." *Scribner's Magazine*, LXXII
(July, 1922), pp. 54-59.
Albert, Frank L., "The Future of the Amusement Park in America." *Billboard*,
March 19, 1910, pp. 20, 21, 86.
"An Automobile Theatre." *Theatre*, XIII (May, 1911), pp. 169, vi.
"An Inveterate Chautauqua Fan." *Scribner's Magazine*, LXXIV (July, 1923),
pp. 119-20.
Appel, Livia, "Early Drama in Minneapolis." *Minnesota History Bulletin*, V
(February, 1923), pp. 43-45.
Arnett, Frank S., "Fifty Years of Uncle Tom." *Munsey's Magazine*, XXVII
(September, 1902), pp. 897-902.
Bagley, Russell E., "Theatrical Entertainment in Pensacola, Florida: 1882-1892."
Southern Speech Journal, XVI (September, 1950), pp. 62-84.
Banks, J. C., "Local Managers' Graft." *Billboard*, September 7, 1907, p. 17.
Baxter, Alice, "Fifty-Five Years on the Stage and Doing One-Night Stands."
Billboard, September 11, 1908, p. 17.
Baxter, Sylvester, "The Trolley in Rural Parks." *Harpers Monthly*, XCVII
(June, 1898), pp. 60-69.
Berquist, Laura, "Show Business in the Sticks." *Coronet Magazine*, XIX
(January, 1946), pp. 121-23.
Berliner, Lawrence, "Press Agents and What They Accomplish." *Billboard*,
August 25, 1906, p. 10.
Bliven, Bruce, "Mother, Home, and Heaven." *New Republic*, XXXVII
(January 9, 1924), pp. 172-75.
Bowen, Elbert R., "The Circus in Early Rural Missouri." *Missouri Historical
Review*, XLVII (October, 1952), pp. 1-17.
Bradley, Alfred, "The Stage and the Provincial Press." New York *Dramatic
Mirror*, February 13, 1897, p. 21.
Bradley, W. F., "Theatre on Wheels." *Harper's Weekly*, LV (August 5, 1911),
p. 24.
Brewer, Clair, "One-Nighter Orgs Plentiful in the Days of Yesteryear." *Billboard*,
September 18, 1948, p. 46.
Bunn, George W., "The Old Chatterton. A Brief History of The Famous Old
Opera House." *Journal of Illinois State Historical Society*, XXXVI
(March, 1943).

Burt, Eliza Logan, As told to Mr. and Mrs. James R. Harvey, "Recollections of the Early Theatre." *Colorado Magazine*, XVII (September, 1940), pp. 161-67.

Carey, John D., "The Circus Press Agent." *Billboard*, April 15, 1911, p. 14.

Carson, William G. B., "Under the Calcium Lights." *Bulletin of the Missouri Historical Society*, XII (July, 1956), pp. 333-57.

Castaigne, Andre, "Strolling Mountebanks." *Harper's Monthly Magazine*, CIII (November, 1901), pp. 841-51.

Castle, Marian Johnson, "Chautauqua, The Intellectual Circus." *Forum*, LXXXVII (June, 1932), pp. 369-74.

Chance, Elbert, "The Great Days of Wilmington's Grand Opera House." *Delaware History*, VIII (September, 1958), pp. 185-99.

Chase, Edwin T., "Forty Years on Main Street." *Iowa Journal of History and Politics*, XXXIV (July, 1935), pp. 227-61.

"Circus Advertising in 1850." *Billboard*, (n.d.).

Clark, Archie L., "John Maguire: Butte's 'Belasco'." *Montana Magazine of History*, II (January, 1952), pp. 33-40.

Coad, Oral Sumner, "The American Theatre in the Eighteenth Century." *South Atlantic Quarterly*, XVII (July, 1918), pp. 190-97.

_____, "Stage and Players in Eighteenth Century America." *Journal of English and Germanic Philology*, XIX, 2 (1920), pp. 201-23.

Colby, Elbridge, "A Supplement on Strollers." *PMLA*, XXXIX (September, 1924), pp. 642-54.

Conlin, James W., "The Merom Bluff Chautauqua." *Indiana Magazine of History*, XXXVI (March, 1940), pp. 23-28.

Conner, William F., "My Impressions of Sarah Bernhardt." *Theatre*, XXII (October, 1915), pp. 172-73, 198.

Cooke, Louis E. and R. M. Harvey, "Handling the Advance." *Billboard*, April 15, 1911, pp. 7, 72.

Cooper, Courtney Ryley, "The Big Show." *Century Magazine*, CVII (December, 1923), pp. 182-94.

Copeland, Ed L., "Jazzing the Drama." *Billboard*, December 18, 1920, p. 37.

Corbett, Elizabeth F., "Early Drama as Represented by Uncle Tom's Cabin." *Drama*, XVI (May, 1926), pp. 285-86.

Court, Ormsby A., "Individuality in Advertising." New York *Dramatic Mirror*, September 8, 1900, p. 14.

Crane, William H., "The Modern Cart of Thespis." *North American Review*, CLIV (April, 1892), pp. 472-79.

Creason, Joe, "Tent Show." *The Courier-Journal Magazine*, Louisville, Kentucky, July 18, 1948, pp. 5-7.

_____, "The Tent Show Carries On." *The Courier-Journal Magazine*, Louisville, Kentucky, August 20, 1961, p. 5.

Davies, Ayres, "Wisconsin, Incubator of the American Circus." *Wisconsin Magazine of History*, XXV (March, 1942), pp. 283-96.

Davis, J. Frank, "Tom Shows." *Scribner's Magazine*, LXXVII (April, 1925), pp. 350-60.

Day, Charles H., "The Press Agent's Antiquity." New York *Dramatic Mirror*, November 25, 1905 p. 13.

Degitz, Dorothy M., "History of the Tabor Opera House in Leadville." *Colorado Magazine*, XIII (May, 1936), pp. 81-89.

Detzer, K. W., "Broadway, R. F. D." *Century Magazine*, CXVI (July, 1928), pp. 311-17.

Dixon, Harry L., "Doff Your Hat to the Tent Show." *Billboard*, March 20, 1926, pp. 9, 13, 218-220.

Donaldson, W. M., "History of Lithography." *Billboard*, December 24, 1910, p. 5.

Dorn-Heft, Dolores, "Toby: The Twilight of a Tradition." *Theatre Arts*, XLII (August, 1958), pp. 52-55, 80.

Dorson, Richard M., "The Yankee on the Stage—A Folk Hero of American Drama." *New England Quarterly*, XII (September, 1940), pp. 467-93.

Douglas, W. A. S., "Pitch Doctors." *American Mercury*, X (February, 1927), pp. 222-26.

Downing, Robert, "Toby." *Theatre Arts*, XXX (November, 1946), pp. 651-55.

Draegert, Eva, "Cultural History of Indianapolis: The Theatre, 1880-1890." *Indiana Magazine of History*, LII (March, 1956), pp. 21-48.

_____ , "The Theatre in Indianapolis Before 1880." *Indiana Magazine of History*, LI (June, 1955), 121-38.

Doble, Charlie, "Who Recalls this Tommer?" *Billboard*, October 23, 1948, p. 50.

Dunbar, Willis Frederick, "The Opera House as a Social Institution in Michigan." *Michigan History Magazine*, XXVI (October-December, 1943), pp. 661-72.

Durang, Charles, "The Philadelphia Stage from the Year 1794 to the Year 1855." Philadelphia *Sunday Dispatch*, 1854-1860. Microfilm, Reel 1.

Eaton, Walter Prichard, "On the One-Night Stand." *American Magazine*, LXXII (June, 1911), pp. 246-56.

_____ , "What's the Matter with the Road?" *American Magazine*, LXXIV (July, 1912), pp. 359-68.

Edgar, Randolph, "Early Minnesota Theatres." *Minnesota History*, IX (March, 1928), p. 33.

Eells, George, "Barn Stormers." *Diners' Club Magazine*, XVI (June, 1965), pp. 48-51.

Ellerbe, Alma and Paul Ellerbe, "The Most American Thing In America." *World's Work*, LXVIII (August, 1924), pp. 440-46.

Emerson, Edwin, Jr., "San Francisco at Play." *Sunset Magazine*, XVII (October, 1906), pp. 319-28.

Emmett, Frank, "Trouping Under Canvas." *Billboard*, December 9, 1911, pp. 24, 97.

Ernst, Alice Henson, "Drama in a Tent." *The Sunday Oregonian Magazine*, Portland, Oregon, December 21, 1952, pp. 8-10.

_____ , "Eugene's Theatres and 'Shows' in Horse and Buggy Days, Part I (1852-1884)." *Oregon Historical Quarterly*, XLIV (June, 1943), pp. 127-39. Part II (September, 1943), pp. 232-48.

Field, Al G., "Inconsistency of Railroad Tariffs Governing Theatrical Traffic." *Billboard*, December 18, 1915, p. 35.

"First Aid to the Circus." *Scientific American*, CXVIII (December 9, 1918), pp. 136-40.

Fletcher, Henry J., "The Doom of the Small Town." *Forum*, XIX (April, 1895), pp. 214-23.

Fox, Roy E., "The Repertoire Show, Under Canvas." *Billboard*, December 22, 1917, pp. 11-12.

French, Strother, "The Great American Forum." *World's Work*, September, 1912, p. 553.

Fuller, Wayne E., "Good Roads and Rural Free Delivery of Mail." *Mississippi Valley Historical Review*, XLII (June, 1955), pp. 67-83.

Glass, James L., "The Growing Popularity of Parks." *Billboard*, March 17, 1906, p. 26.

Grau, Robert, "The Vaudeville of Today and Tomorrow." *Billboard*, October 28, 1911, p. 4.

Hallock, E. S., "The American Circus." *Century Magazine*, LXX (August, 1905), pp. 568-85.

Hamilton, Clayton, "Melodrama, Old and New." *Bookman*, XXXIII (May, 1911), pp. 309-14.

Harger, Charles M., "An Era of Thrift in the Middle West." *World's Work*, V (February, 1903), pp. 3091-93.

Harper, Robert D., "Theatrical Entertainment in Early Omaha." *Nebraska History*, XXXVI (June, 1955), pp. 93-104.

Hartt, Rollin Lunde, "The Amusement Park." *Atlantic Monthly*, XCIX (May, 1907), pp. 667-77.

Herbert, Carl, "The Front of the House: I. Protecting the Cash." New York *Dramatic Mirror*, July 21, 1900, p. 14.

_____, "The Front of the House: II. The 'Actor-Owner's' Interests." New York *Dramatic Mirror*, July 28, 1900, p. 8.

_____, "The Front of the House: III. The Advance Sale." New York *Dramatic Mirror*, August 4, 1900, p. 3.

Herne, James A., "The Old Stock Days in the Theatre." *Arena*, VI (September, 1892), pp. 401-16.

"Hey Rube." *Nation*, CXXIX (November 6, 1929), p. 513.

High, Fred, "Chautauqua Growth." *Billboard*, March 20, 1920, pp. 16-17, 204.

_____, "The Circus and the Chautauqua." *Billboard*, December 22, 1917, pp. 14-15.

Hill, Clare Maynard, "Sartorial Splendors in Vaudeville." *Billboard*, November 29, 1913, pp. 34, 138.

Hollister, Katherine Stevens, "The Theatre in Jackson, 1890-1910." *Journal of Mississippi History*, XVII (April, 1955), pp. 127-34.

Hood, Charles Newton, "The One-Night Stand." *Scribner's Monthly*, LXXI (March, 1927), pp. 285-94.

_____, "Running a One-Night Stand in 'the Sticks'." *Theatre*, XLVIII (August, 1928), pp. 15, 52.

Horton, C. L., "Railroads and the Profession." *Billboard*, December 11, 1909, pp. 23, 66.

Howard, Randall R., "Chautauqua Invades the West." *Sunset*, XXXX (May, 1918), pp. 49-50.

Howe, Edgar, "Ed Howe on Sarah Bernhardt." *Kansas Historical Quarterly*, May, 1950, pp. 209-12.
"How the Circus Dodges the Railroad Blockade." *Literary Digest*, LVI (March 16, 1918), pp. 87-88.
Hutton, James S., "The Amusement Park: American Institution." *Billboard*, March 19, 1910, pp. 25, 84.
Jensen, Andrew F., "Two Decades of Trouping in Minnesota." *Minnesota History*, XXVIII (June, 1947), pp. 97-119.
Johnson, Winifred, "Medicine Show." *Southwest Review*, XXI (July, 1936), pp. 390-99.
Kaye, Joseph, "Drama Under the Big Top." *Theatre*, XI (March, 1930), pp. 31, 68, 70.
Kelm, William E., "The People's Theatre." *Palimpsest*, IX (March, 1928), pp. 89-105.
King, Floyd, "What the Press Agent Represents." *Billboard*, March 22, 1913, pp. 39, 146.
Krone, Charles A., "Recollections of an Old Actor." *Missouri Historical Society Collections*:
III (January, 1908), pp. 53-70; III (April, 1908), pp. 170-82; III (April, 1911), pp. 275-306; III (April, 1911), pp. 423-36; IV, 1 (1912), pp. 104-20; IV, 2 (1913), pp. 209-33; IV, 3 (1914), pp. 323-51; IV, 4 (1923), pp. 423-63.
Lawrence, John, "Jesse James vs. East Lynne." *Billboard*, March 22, 1919, pp. 33, 208, 209.
Lawrence, W. J., "Early Playbills." New York *Dramatic Mirror*, June 3, 1905, p. 14.
Lee, Albert, "The Moving of a Modern Caravan." *Harper's Weekly*, XXXIX (May 25, 1895), pp. 493-95.
Locke, Will H., "Gay '90's Airdomes Ace Summer Spots for Repsters." *Billboard*, November 6, 1948, p. 53.
"The Lounger," *Putman's Monthly and the Critic*, I (November, 1906), p. 214.
Lucey, Thomas Elmore, "Chautauqua, The Show With a Conscience." *Billboard*, March 24, 1917, pp. 31, 214.
Mahan, Bruce E., "At the Opera House." *Palimpsest*, V (November, 1924), pp. 408-23.
Malin, James C., "Traveling Theatre in Kansas: The James A. Lord Chicago Dramatic Company, 1869-1871." *Kansas Historical Quarterly*, Part I (Autumn, 1956), pp. 298-323; Part II (Winter, 1957), pp. 401-38.
Mansen, George J., "The Making of the Theatre: I. The Building." New York *Dramatic Mirror*, June 20, 1896, p. 14.
_____, "The Making of the Theatre: II. The Scenery." New York *Dramatic Mirror*, June 27, 1896, p. 14.
_____, "The Making of the Theatre: III. The Stage Director." New York *Dra Mirror*, July 11, 1896, p. 14.
_____, "The Making of the Theatre: IV. The Lighting." New York *Dramatic Mirror*, July 25, 1896, p. 4.
_____, "The Making of the Theatre: V. Stage Mechanism and Stage Effects." New York *Dramatic Mirror*, August 1, 1896, p. 4.

_____, "The Making of the Theatre: VI. The Business Management." New York *Dramatic Mirror*, August 15, 1896, p. 4

_____, "The Making of the Theatre: VII. The Front of the House." New York *Dramatic Mirror*, August 29, 1896, p. 4.

_____, "The Making of the Theatre: IX. The Traveling Combination." New York *Dramatic Mirror*, October 31, 1896, p. 23.

_____, "The Making of the Theatre: X. The Costumes." New York *Dramatic Mirror*, November 7, 1896, p. 4.

Macrosson, Isaac F., "Sawdust and the Gold Dust, the Earnings of the Circus People." *Bookman*, XXXI (June, 1910), pp. 402-10.

Mawson, Harry P., "In Stock." *Theatre*, XVII (July, 1913), pp. 26-30.

May, Earl Chapin, "Our Canvas Broadway." *Country Gentlemen*, May, 1931, pp. 16, 17, 95.

Mickel, Jere C., "The Genesis of Toby." *Journal of American Folklore*, LXXX (October-December, 1967), 334-40.

Miles, Carlton, "Doubling in Brass." *Theatre Arts*, X (October, 1926), pp. 685-88.

Mishler, John, "A Letter from John Mishler." New York *Dramatic Mirror*, August 12, 1893, p. 9.

_____, "The Theatre Commercially Considered." New York *Dramatic Mirror*, June 30, 1910, p. 2; July 7, 1900, p. 9; July 14, 1900, p. 8.

Moffett, Cleveland, "How the Circus is Put Up and Taken Down." *McClure's Magazine*, V (June, 1895), pp. 49-61.

Moffett, Walter, "First Theatrical Activities in Arkansas." *Arkansas Historical Quarterly*, XII (Winter, 1953), pp. 327-32.

Moody, Richard and A. M. Drummond, "The Hit of the Century: Uncle Tom's Cabin." *Educational Theatre Journal*, IV (1952), pp. 315-22.

Moore, Frank E., "As I See It." *Billboard*, February 2, 1924, p. 28.

Morris, Joe Alex, "Corniest Show on the Road." *Saturday Evening Post*, CCXXVIII (September 17, 1955), 30-31, 60-62, 70.

Murray, Kenneth, "Next Week—East Lynne." *Spot*, I (July, 1941), pp. 20-22.

Naeseth, Henriette, "Drama in Early Deadwood, 1876-1879." *American Literature*, X (November, 1938), pp. 289-312.

"Nature's Cataclysm in San Francisco." *Theatre*, VI (June, 1906), pp. 146-47, xii.

Nealand, Walter D., "10-20-30—and Up (the Ladder)." *Billboard*, November 30, 1940, pp. 29, 88.

Nobles, Milton, "Some Unwritten Stage History." *Theatre*, XXIV (July, 1916), pp. 31-32.

"Old Days of Sawdust and Spangles." *Literary Digest*, LV (August 18, 1917), pp. 50-53.

O'Neil, Nance, "One-Night Stands of America." *Harper's Weekly*, LIV (December 3, 1910), p. 23.

Perrigo, Lynn, "The First Two Decades of Central City Theatricals." *Colorado Magazine*, IX (July, 1934), pp. 141-52.

Peterman, H. A., "The 'Tab' Show." *Billboard*, December 22, 1917, pp. 21, 160, 161.

Phillips, E. Bryant, "Interurban Projects in Nebraska." *Nebraska History*, XXX (June 19, 1919), pp. 163-82.

Popkin, Zelda F., "The Tent Show Turns to Sex." *Outlook and Independent*, CLVI (September 24, 1930), pp. 128-30.

Pringle, Henry F., "Chautauqua in the Jazz Age." *American Mercury*, XVI (January, 1929), pp. 85-93.

Ranck, Edwin Carty, "What's Wrong with the Road?" *Theatre*, XXVI (October, 1917, p. 218.

Ranney, Omar, "Forever Toby." *Theatre Arts*, August, 1953, pp. 73, 95.

Reichmann, Felix, "Amusements in Lancaster, 1750-1940." *Lancaster County Historical Society*, XLV (1941), pp. 25-55.

Reyam, "The Amusement Park." *Billboard*, March 19, 1910, pp. 12, 13, 82.

Rial, Jay, "Evolution of the Circus." *Billboard*, December 22, 1917, pp. 12, 13, 164.

Robinson, Clyde, "Tennessee Goes to the Show." *Theatre Arts*, XVI (April, 1932), pp. 316-22.

Robinson, Fayette Lodawick, "Dilly Fay, the Clown: a Reminiscence of a Showman's Life." New York *Clipper*, February 17, 1872, p. 364.

Robinson, Gil, "The Circus Life in the Early Days." *Billboard*, December 9, 1911, pp. 22, 72.

Rogers, A. R., "Advice to Street Railway Managers of Parks." *Billboard*, March 23, 1901, p. 17.

"Rose Melville—The Feminine Denman Thompson." *Theatre*, VIII (January, 1908), pp. 28-29.

Row, Arthur William, "Acting in Tents in Chautauqua." *Poet Lore*, XXXVI (Summer, 1925), pp. 222-23.

Royle, Edwin Milton, "The Vaudeville Theatre." *Scribner's Magazine*, XXVI (October, 1899), pp. 485-95.

Ruhl, Arthur, "Ten-Twenty-Thirty." *Outlook*, XCVIII (August 19, 1911), pp. 886-91.

Rulfs, Donald J., "The Professional Theatre in Wilmington, 1870-1900." *North Carolina Historical Review*, XXVIII (July, 1951), pp. 316-31.

_____, "The Professional Theatre in Wilmington, 1900-1930." *North Carolina Historical Review*, XXVIII (October, 1951), pp. 463-85.

_____, "The Theatre in Ashville from 1879 to 1931." *North Carolina Historical Review*, XXXVI (October, 1959), 429-41.

Ryan, Pat M., "Hallo's Opera House: Pioneer Theatre of Lincoln, Nebraska." *Nebraska History*, XLV (December, 1964), pp. 323-30.

"Sarah Bernhardt's Triumphant Tour in the West." *Theatre*, VI (May, 1906), p. 115.

Saxby, Howard, "A Thespian Reminiscence." *Billboard*, December 5, 1908, p. 15.

Sayre, Hal, "Early Central City Theatricals and Other Reminiscences." *Colorado Magazine*, VI (March, 1929), pp. 47-52.

Schick, Joseph S., "The American Theatre in Davenport, Iowa." *Palimpsest*, January, 1950, pp. 8-9.

Skinner, Charles M., "The Electric Car." *Atlantic Monthly*, LXXXIX (June, 1902), pp. 799-808.

Slout, L. Verne, "The Chautauqua Drama." *Lyceum Magazine*, (April, 1923), pp. 19-20.

Smith, Harry James, "The Melodrama." *Atlantic Monthly*, XCIX (March, 1907), pp. 320-28.

Smith, John Harrington, "Tony Lumpkin and the Country Booby Type in Antecedent English Comedy." *PMLA*, LVIII (December, 1943), pp. 1038-49.

Spitzer, Marian, "Ten-Twenty-Thirty, the Passing of the Popular-Priced Circuit." *Saturday Evening Post*, CXCVIII (August 22, 1925), pp. 40, 42, 48.

Stallings, Roy, "The Drama in Southern Illinois, 1865-1900." *Journal of the Illinois State Historical Society*, XXXIII (June, 1940), pp. 190-202.

Stevens, George W., Sr. (Dr. Judd), "The Old Wagon Days with Theatrical Companies." New York *Dramatic Mirror*, December 20, 1902, Christmas Issue, p. x.

Stout, Wesley Winans, "Little Eva is Seventy-Five." *Saturday Evening Post*, CC (October 8, 1927), pp. 10-11, 191, 193-94, 197-98, 201.

_____ , "Med Show." *Saturday Evening Post*, CCII, (September 14, 1929), pp. 12, 13, 166, 169, 173, 174.

Stow, Charles, "The Pioneers of 'the American Circus'." *Theatre*, V (August, 1905), pp. 192-94.

Sweet, Oney Fred, "An Iowa County Seat." *Iowa Journal of History and Politics*, XXXVIII (October, 1940), pp. 339-407.

Talley, T. H., "The Chautauqua, an American Achievement." *World's Work*, XLII (June, 1921), pp. 172-84.

Thaler, Alwin, "Strolling Players and Provincial Drama After Shakespeare." *PMLA*, XXXVII (June, 1922), pp. 243-80.

"The Theatre Everywhere." *The Theatre*, VI (April, 1906), pp. xviii-xx.

"A Theatre with a 5,000,000 Audience." *World's Work*, XX (May, 1910), p. 12876.

"A Theatrical Press Agent's Confession and Apology." *Independent*, LIX (July 27, 1905), pp. 191-96.

Tilden, Freeman, "What the Farmer Really Looks Like." *Country Gentleman*, LXXXVI (July 2, 1921), pp. 6-7.

Todd, William, "Are the Railroads Hurting Us?" *Billboard*, March 27, 1915, pp. 11, 170.

Tower, Grace Hortense, "With Sarah Bernhardt on Her Tour in California." *Theatre*, VI (July, 1906), pp. 181-83, vi.

"The Tribe of 'Prairie Actors'." New York *Dramatic Mirror*, August 8, 1896, p. 9.

Vail, R. W. G., "This Way to the Big Top." *New York Historical Society Bulletin*, XXIX (July, 1945), pp. 137-59.

Veblin, Thorstein, "The Country Town." *Freeman*, VII (July 11, 1923), pp. 417-20; (July 18, 1923), pp. 440-43.

Wamack, Thomas, "Some Observations About Press Agents." *Billboard*, April 3, 1909, p. 18.

Ware, Helen, "The Road." *Theatre*, XXVI (July, 1917), pp. 26, 52.
Wayne, Donald, "Entertainment." *Holiday*, III (June, 1948), pp. 14, 16, 19.
"What Has Become of Uncle Tom's Cabin." *American Playwright*, III (August, 1914), pp. 264-66.
Willey, Day Allen, "The Open-Air Amusement Park." *Theatre*, X (July, 1909), pp. 18-19.
_____ , "The Trolley-Park." *Cosmopolitan*, XXXIII (July, 1902), pp. 265-72.
Wilson, E. E., "Canvas and Culture." *Outlook*, CXXXI (August 9, 1922), pp. 598-600.
Wilson, W. L., "The Tented Theatre." *Billboard*, March 23, 1912, pp. 34, 84.
Woods, Donald Z., "Playhouse for Pioneers: the Story of the Pence Opera House." *Minnesota History*, XXXIII (Winter, 1952), pp. 169-78.
Woosey, Bill, "Good Clean Entertainment." *The Nashville Tennessean Magazine*, May 22, 1949, pp. 5-8.
Zilboorg, Gregory, "Chautauqua and the Drama." *Drama*, XII (October-November, 1921), pp. 16-18.
_____ , "The Stageless Road." *Drama*, XI (August-September, 1921) pp. 395-96, 401.

E. PLAYS

The British Theatre; or, a Collection of Plays Which Were Acted, At Drury Lane, Covent Garden, and Haymarket, XXV. Biographical and Critical remarks by Mrs. Inchbald. London, Longman, Jurst, Rees, and Orme, 1808.
Black, Clarence, *Jesse James*. Mimeographed copy. Copyrighted 1909.
Compston, Nelson, *Lena Rivers*. Mimeographed copy. Copyrighted 1909.
_____ , *Under Arizona Skies*. Mimeographed copy. Copyrighted 1910.
_____ , and W. C. Herman, *Won by Waiting*. Typewritten copy. Copyrighted 1912.
Crawley, George J., *The Girl of the Flying X*. Typewritten copy. Copyrighted 1916.
Dunlap, William, "Darby's Return," *America's Lost Plays*, XXI, Walter J. Meserve and William R. Reardon (eds.). Bloomington, Indiana, Indiana University Press, 1969.
Harrison, Charles F., *The Awakening of John Slater*. Typewritten copy. Copyrighted 1914.
_____ , *The Only Road*. Mimeographed copy.
_____ , *Saintly Hypocrites and Honest Sinners*. Typewritten copy. Copyrighted 1915.
Hayes, Charles Sumner, *The Natural Law*. Typewritten copy. Copyrighted 1914.
Herman, W. C., *Call of the Woods*. Mimeographed copy. Copyrighted 1912.
_____ , *Clouds and Sunshine*. Typewritten copy. Copyrighted 1911.
Lamson, Ernest, *Tobe Hoxie*. Copy of manuscript at the University of Chicago Library. Copyrighted 1900.

Morton, Thomas and J. M. Morton, *All That Glitters is Not Gold.* New York, Harold Roorbach, 1899.
Phelps, Pauline and Marion Short, *The Girl From Out Yonder.* Mimeo. Ⓒ 1913.
Reid, James Halleck, *Knobs O' Tennessee.* Typewritten copy. Copyrighted 1899.
Slemons, Freda, *Sweetest Girl in Dixie.* Typewritten copy. Copyrighted 1906.
Smith, Charles Jay (probable author), *Over the Hills to the Poor House.* Mimeographed copy. Copyrighted 1904.
Smith, Winchell and John E. Hazzard, *Turn to the Right.* New York: Samuel French, 1916.
Tyler, Royall, "The Contrast," *Dramas from the American Theatre, 1762-1909.* Richard Moody, (ed.). Cleveland, World Publishing Company, 1966.

F. REFERENCE BOOKS

Dramatic Compositions Copyrighted in the United States, 1870-1916. Two Volumes. Washington, Government Printing Office, 1918.
Hartnoll, Phyllis (ed.), *The Oxford Companion to the Theatre.* London, Oxford University Press, 1951.
Nagler, A. M., *A Source Book in Theatrical History.* New York, Dover Publications, Inc., 1952.
Odell, George C. D., *Annals of the New York Stage.* 15 vols. New York, Columbia University Press, 1927-49.
Wemyss, Francis Courtney, *Chronology of the American Stage from 1752-1852.* New York, 1852.
Yearbook of the United States Department of Agriculture, 1916. Washington, Government Printing Office, 1917.
Yearbook of the United States Department of Agriculture, 1921. Washington, Government Printing Office, 1922.

G. TAPED INTERVIEWS

Arnold, Bert. Interviewed by James V. Davis, September 6, 1966.
Brown, Frank L. Interviewed by Harvey Friedman, November 30, 1969.
Carlstrom, O'Lee. Interviewed by Harvey Friedman, November 30, 1969.
Davis, Ann B. Interviewed by James V. Davis, September 6, 1966.
_____. Interviewed by Harvey Friedman, November 30, 1969.
Davis, Juanita. Interviewed by Muner Hanafi, November 30, 1969.
Dexter, Bert. Interviewed by James V. Davis, September 6, 1966.
Fair, Beula. Interviewed by Harvey Friedman, November 30, 1969.
Forrest, Guy. Interviewed by William Slout, September 2, 1967.
Gentry, Maude. Interviewed by Harvey Friedman, November 30, 1969.
Gordinier, Otis. Interviewed by William Slout, September 29, 1967.
Gray, Ermin. Interviewed by James V. Davis, September 6, 1966.
_____. Interviewed by William Slout, September 2, 1967.
Grossman, Moritz A. Interviewed by Muner Hanafi, November 30, 1969.

Lacy, Leo. Interviewed by James V. Davis, September 6, 1966.
Mickel, Jere C. Interviewed by William Slout, September 8, 1966.
Murphy, Horace. Interviewed by William Slout, September 20, 1967.
_____. Interviewed by William Slout, September 25, 1967.
North, Mary. Interviewed by William Slout, May 1, 1965.
North, Ted. Interviewed by William Slout, May 1, 1965.
Olson, Cliff. Interviewed by Harvey Friedman, November 30, 1969.
Pitcaithley, Al. Interviewed by William Slout, September 10, 1966.
Rosier, Harold. Interviewed by James V. Davis, September 6, 1966.
Schaffner, Neil. Interviewed by William Slout, September 1, 1967.
_____. Interviewed by William Slout, September 2, 1967.
Sharpe, Ernest Jack. Interviewed by William Slout, June 25, 1967.
Taylor, Leona. Interviewed by Harvey Friedman, November 30, 1969.
Wilkes, Mason. Interviewed by William Slout, September 1, 1967.
Wortham, Charles. Interviewed by William Slout, September 1, 1967.

G. UNPUBLISHED MATERIALS

Brian, George, "A History of Theatrical Activities in Baton Rouge from1900 to 1923." Unpublished Master's thesis, Louisiana State University, June, 1951.
Clark, Larry Dale, "Toby Shows: A Form of American Popular Theatre." Unpublished dissertation, University of Illinois, 1963.
Gray, Wallace Allison, "The Professional Theatre in Alexandria, Louisiana, 1822-1920." Unpublished Master's thesis, Louisiana State University, 1951.
Latchaw, Truly Trousdale, "The Trousdale Brothers' Theatrical Companies from 1896 to 1915." Unpublished Master's thesis, University of Minnesota, 1948.
Snyder, Sherwood, III, "The Toby Shows." Doctoral dissertation, University of Minnesota, 1966.
Teague, Oran, "The Professional Theatre in Rural Louisiana." Unpublished Master's thesis, Louisiana State University, 1952.

INDEX

Clark, Larry Dale, 91
Clark's Comedians, 118n
Clifton Comedy Co., 118n
Clouds and Sunshine, 77, 83, 90-97
Clover Dale, 120n
Cobler of Preston, The, 121n
Col. Bailey, 77
Colby Family, 15
College Widow, The, 61
Collins, Ulric, 61
Col. Manly, 87
Colonial Stock Co., 118n
Comedy of Errors, 55
Comical Countess, The, 16
Committee of National Defense, 65
Compston, Nelson, 77
Compton-Plumb Stock Co., 118n
Conger and Santo, 118n
Conner, William F., 58, 59
Contrast, The, 86-88
Convict's Daughter, The, 15
Cooper and Bailey Circus, 46
Copeland, Ed L., 94
Copeland Brothers Stock Co. (Ed L.), 45, 117n, 118n
Corrine Blair, 81
Cosgrave, Luke, 21, 65
Costello's Circus and Menagerie (Dan), 67
Cotton Blossom Show Boat, 93
Country Squire, The, 121n
Country Wife, The, 81
County Fair, The, 29
Coup, William Cameron, 38
Craig, Charles, 55
Craig, Lois, 55
Crane and Company's Great Oriental Circus, 104
Crane, William H., 7
Crawford's Comedians, 45, 117n, 118n
Crawley, George J., 76
Crawley's Comedians, 118n
Crisp Dramatic Troupe (W. H.), 17
Criterion Stock Co., 117n
Cuckoo Song, 17
Culhane's Minstrels, 6

Curley Stock Co. (Bessie), 117n
Curtis-McDonald's Comedians, 118n
Cythia, 17

D

Daisy Farm, 17
Dalley Stock Co., 118n
Dangers of a Great City, 115n
Darby, 86-88, 121n
Darby's Return, 86, 88, 121n
Daughter of the Regiment, The, 6
Dave Hughes, 78
Davidge, William, 89
Davis, Charles L., 113n
Davis, James, 112
Davis, Juanita, 112
Deacon Malcolm, 75
Deacon Stromberg, 75
Deacon Tillinger, 79
Dean, Frank J., 20
De Gafferelly Co. (Marie), 51
De Lussan, Henry, 8
Deming Theatre Co. (Lawrence), 118n
Demorest Stock Co. (Robert and Ona), 51, 118n
D' Erina, Rosa, 6
Derious, Edwin, 66
D' Este, Helen, 17
Detroit *News,* 20
deus ex machina, 83
De Voss, Flora, 18, 22
De Voss Repertoire Co. (Flora), 118n
Dimple, 87
Diomos, 85
Dockstader's Minstrels, 6
Doctor's Prescription, 120n
Dogberry, 85
Doherty, Frank J., 99
Dolly Bond, 72
Don Caesar de Bazan, 17
Don Quixote, 84
Dora Thorne, 71
Doris Keene, 78

Leffingwell, Myron, 77
Le Grande Duchess, 25
Lehr Stock Co. (Ina and Betty), 51
Lena Rivers, 71, 114n
Lewis, John C., 7
Lewis Stock Co. (William F.), 69, 117n, 118n, 119n
Lightnin', 56
Lightnin' Bill Jones, 119n
Liliputian Opera Co., 6
Lincon Square Theatre, N.Y., 33
Lindsey Stock Co. (Lester), 119n
Little Eva, 19, 21
Loan of a Lover, A, 16
Locke, Will H., 4, 5
London Assurance, 17
London Hermit, The, 121n
Lone Star Minstrels, 50
Lone Star Ranch, The, 120n
Long's Associated Players (Guy E.), 45, 119n
Loraine, Robert, 61
Lord Dramatic Co. (James A.), 16
Love in a Camp, 121n
Love of a Thief, The, 120n
Lowery Brothers, 119n
Ludlow, Noah, 12
Luff, Theodore, 116n
Lun Slater, 76
Lynwood, 116n
Lyons, Lillian, 18

M

Mac Millan, Dan, 93
Mc Allister, Miss Phosa, 17
Mc Cormick, Langdon, 83, 93, 97
Mc Cutcheon, George Barr, 71
Mc Farland, John, 16
Mc Kinley and Wall Co., 27
Mac Stock Co., 119n
Mac-Taff Co., 119n
Madame Fickle, 88
Maddock's Park Players, 119n
Majestic Theatre, N.Y., 33
Manhattan Theatre, N.Y., 33

Man in the Iron Mask, The, 17
Man of Mystery, The, 21
Mansfield, Richard, 58, 59
Manville Brothers, 119n
Maritana, 25
Marjorie Morgan, 96
Marlowe, Julia, 61
Married Rake, The, 16
Marshall Players, 119n
Martin, Ira Jack, 56
Mary Fletcher, 75
Ma Slater, 76
Mason and Imson's Pavilion Theatre, 117n
Mason, Dick, 51
Mason-Williams Co. (Dick and Fanny), 51
Master and Man, 15
Mathes, Clara, 18
Mathews and Bulgar, 72
Maxam and Sights' Comedians, 50, 117n
Maxwell, George, 115n
May, Earl Chapin, 38
Meek, Donald, 93
Melting Pot, The, 56
Melville, Bert, 100
Melville, Ida, 72, 119n
Melville, Rose, 72-73, 119n
Melville's Comedians (Bert), 100, 119n
Melville Stock Co. (Emilie), 16
Menken, Ada B., 114n
Meredith, E. E., 15, 23
Metropolis Theatre, N.Y., 93
Mexicana, 61
Mickel, J. C., 91, 92
Miller, William,
Miller Brothers, 119n
Millerites, 39
Miller Stock Co., 117n
Mills, Charles T., 74
Milton Comedy Co., 107
Minnelli Brothers Stock Co., 46, 117n, 119n
Mishler, John, 32